A BEGINNER'S **ART** GUIDE

Illuminated lettering

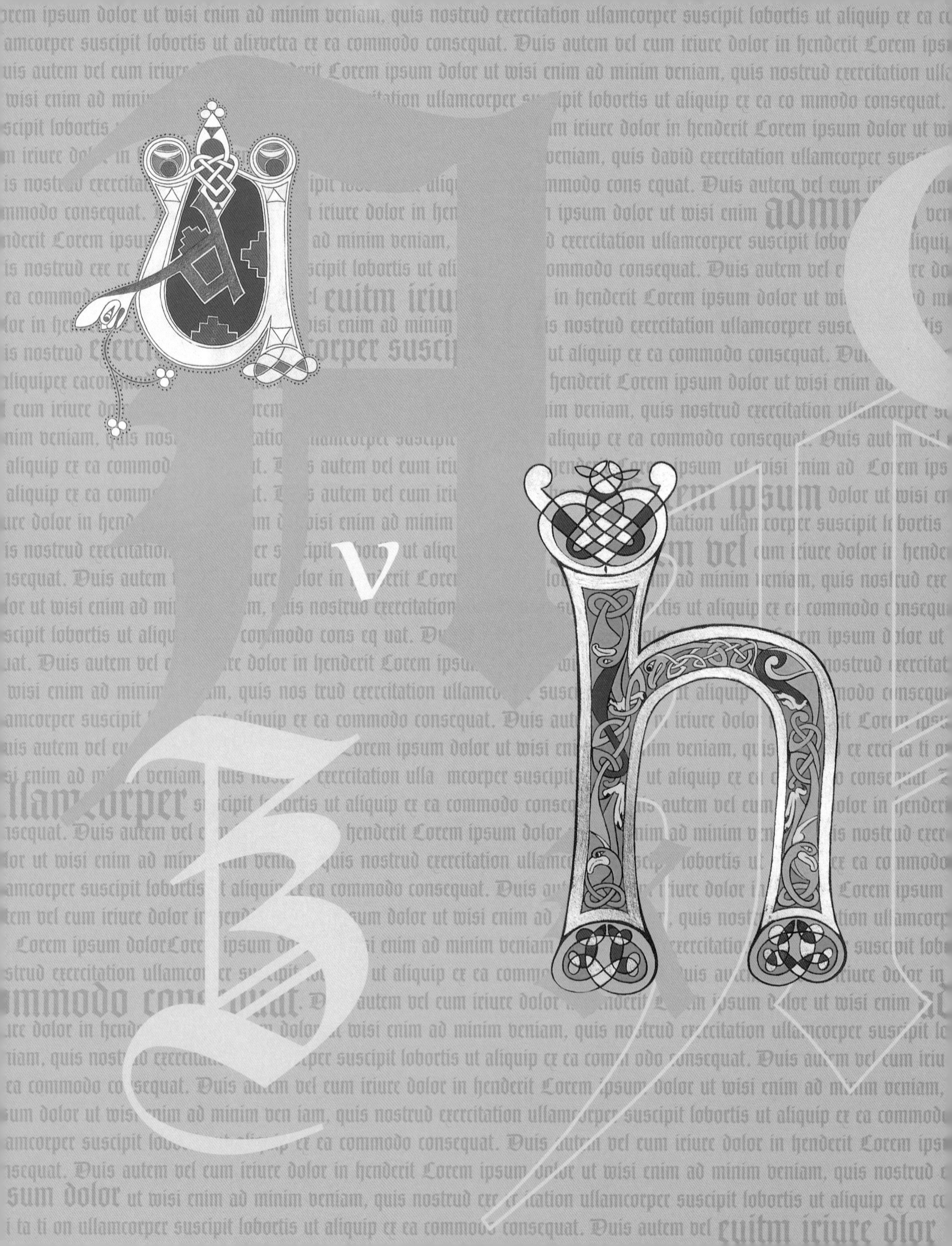
V

A BEGINNER'S **ART** GUIDE

Illuminated lettering

THEY WILL HAVE TO
BEAT
THEIR SWORDS
INTO PLOWSHARES
and their spears
into pruning
shears. They will
not lift up sword,
nation against nation, neither will
they learn war anymore. Isaiah 2:4

Marie Lynskey

D&S
BOOKS

First published in 2001 by D&S Books

© 2001 D&S Books

D&S Books
Cottage Meadow, Bocombe,
Parkham, Bideford
Devon, England
EX39 5PH

e-mail us at:-
enquiries.dspublishing@care4free.net

This edition printed 2001

ISBN 1-903327-15-6

Editorial Director: Sarah King
Editor: Clare Haworth-Maden
Project Editor: Judith Millidge
Photographer: Paul Forrester
Designer: Axis Design

Distributed in the UK & Ireland by
Bookmart Limited
Desford Road
Enderby
Leicester LE9 5AD

Distributed in Australia by
Herron Books
39 Commercial Road
Fortitude Valley
Queensland 4006

1 3 5 7 9 10 8 6 4 2

CONTENTS

Introduction

Looking at some of the fine illuminated manuscripts that are on display in various parts of the world , with their richly decorated gilded letters and texts, will prove a real inspiration for anybody who has an artistic bent and knowledge of calligraphy. The British Library in the St Pancras district of London, for example, is blessed with a wealth of such manuscripts, many of which are in a good state of repair and still exhibit much of their original glory. Other museums around the world boast some equally fine examples, in particular the incredibly complex Book of Kells that can be seen at Trinity College, Dublin, Ireland, and the Winchester Bible, which is housed in Winchester Cathedral, Hampshire, England. Many beautiful manuscripts can also be seen in the J Paul Getty Museum in Malibu, California, USA, as well as in many other national libraries' collections, such as those of Sweden, in Stockholm, and of Austria, in Vienna. Wherever possible, original sources have been given for all of the examples of illuminated letters that appear in this book, which are all reproductions of the original works, as well as the repositories where the manuscripts are currently kept (these change from time to time, however, so before making a long trip to see a specific piece, always check that it has neither been sent away on a long loan nor been permanently re-homed).

An examination of the methods that were used to produce these fine works reveals the use of materials and equipment from times long past, when mass production was not possible. Instead, time and effort were needed to create books of incredible richness and complexity, whose purpose was to glorify God, to satisfy rich men and to educate the privileged. Such materials can still be procured, and the methods of construction that the original scribes used will be illustrated and described in this book to enable the student to create contemporary works of a similar nature.

The history of illuminated letters

During the period known as antiquity, before the decline of the Roman Empire during the fifth century, lettering was principally unadorned. It wasn't until the spread of Christianity – which Emperor Constantine had established as Rome's official religion in AD 311 – throughout the Western world that the importance of the written word began to increase as a result of the desire to transmit and reinforce the word of God. Books were therefore produced in increasing numbers by means of the only method available: copying them by hand from borrowed texts. It is in the early Christians' efforts both to increase the stature of their holy books and to reflect the reverence in which they were held that we can see the beginning of the art of illumination.

Illuminated letters are chiefly found in books of the scriptures. For the origins of the texts that were used in early illuminated works, we have to go back to about the year 382, when, on his arrival in Rome after years of travelling, St Jerome was commissioned by Pope Damasus to edit and revise the old Latin texts of the four gospels. As well as complying using the available Greek texts, Jerome went further and studied Hebrew to enable him to revise the books of the Old Testament. He produced three versions of the Hebrew text, two of which are written side by side in parts of the Winchester Bible, although in some other works all three translations appear together. Until the Reformation, Jerome's Latin text (which was known as the Vulgate), was used by the Christian Church throughout the West for most medieval bibles. Indeed, it is still used by the Roman Catholic Church today.

Figure 1: 'T', Book of Kells.

Scripts of the Dark Ages

The Germanic peoples who settled in, or conquered, parts of the western Roman Empire formed isolated settlements. Throughout what are termed the Dark Ages, such new states as the Frankish kingdoms, Visigothic Spain, Ostrogothic and Lombardic Italy, as well as Anglo-Saxon England, emerged. And from the pens and brushes of the scribes and artists who were working in the isolated religious centres of these lands blossomed superb, illuminated texts in different styles.

The scribes of Britain and Ireland were responsible for some of the earliest – as well as the finest – illuminated works of the Dark Ages. The conversion of the Anglo-Saxons to Christianity occurred in AD 597, when Pope Gregory the Great sent St Augustine to Canterbury to accomplish this end. The style of the work produced as a result has become known as insular, and the scribes and scholars that used the insular style influenced the work of early illuminators throughout the rest of Europe.

It was mainly monks who produced the illuminated manuscripts of this time. The monasteries were centres of learning and culture,

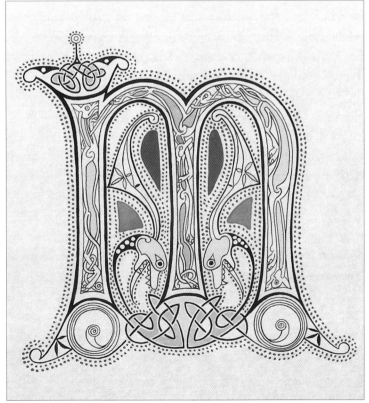

Figure 2: 'Q', Lindisfarne Gospels.

and monks taught young men of good families such skills as they knew. Newly founded monasteries, or those whose monks were less skilled, requested books from those that were well established. Indeed, some monasteries specialised in producing books for other communities, which were often passed from monastery to monastery so that new generations of monks could learn the skills of writing and illumination.

Figure 1 shows an illustration from the Book of Kells. Although the origins of this impressive manuscript are uncertain, it is thought to have been produced in either Ireland or Northumbria during the eighth century. The initial 'T', shown here, commences text which leads into a page full of rich, Celtic patterns and intricate detailing. The Lindisfarne Gospels (Figure 2), which is currently on display at the British Library, was produced in Lindisfarne, in the north of England, at the end of the seventh century. A wonderful example of illuminated work, the Lindisfarne Gospels is full of very complex, interwoven decoration consisting of animals and birds arranged in beautifully stylised patterns. Although not all insular manuscripts reached the same high standard as the Book of Kells or the Lindisfarne Gospels, they all shared incredible complex, imaginative designs. And even though the years have robbed them of some of their original strength of colour, the rich hues and delicacy of some of the paintings that they contain remain stunning to behold.

Another wonderful piece of illumination is the *Codex Aureus*, which is thought to have been written in Canterbury during the mid-eighth century, and can today be admired at Stockholm's Kungliga Biblioteket. It is an incredible work that boasts large amounts of gilding, as well as intricate patterns. A marginal note in the book, written in beautiful, Anglo-Saxon script, records that during the ninth century one Aldorman Aelfred paid a ransom of gold to pagan Norsemen in order to procure it.

Not all of the illuminated books of the period were based on the scriptures, however. Books on astronomy began to be produced from the mid-ninth century, which were important for determining the dates of religious festivals. Herbals have also survived. These were manuscripts that were illuminated with paintings of plants, while their descriptions and uses, along with other medical details, such as operations and attempted cures, were conveyed by both the

text and illustrations. Another type of illuminated book was the bestiary, whose origins lay in Greek writings and biblical tales, which contained details of both real and imaginary creatures. Bestiaries served as books of instruction, and although the texts were generally illustrated with representations of plants or creatures, they contained few illuminated letters.

The Carolingian script

Under the patronage of Charlemagne, the king of the Franks who was created the first Holy Roman Emperor in AD 800, learning and the arts flourished. The many fine illuminated works that were produced during his reign were written in the Carolingian style that was named after the emperor. The appearance of the manuscripts writ-

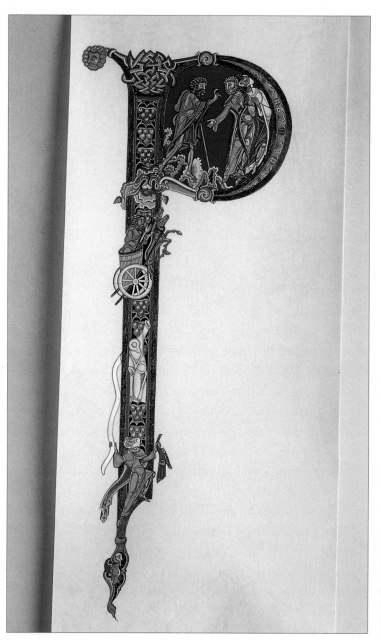

Figure 3: 'P', Winchester Bible.

ten in the Carolingian style differed greatly from those of preceding styles. The precise, minuscule lettering of the text was accompanied by single, large and well-defined illuminated letters, while additional words in title pieces were picked out in simple, coloured, capital letters. Pages of Carolingian text did not have the busy, cluttered appearance of Celtic manuscripts, but instead displayed a composed dignity and sense of order that remained popular for several centuries.

Alcuin of York, an English scholar who was closely associated with Charlemagne, used the Carolingian script to write a text of the Latin Bible that was subsequently used as a model for the production of many other illustrated bibles. Because of their great size and weight, such large bibles, which were intended to be read aloud from a lectern, were usually bound into several volumes. The initial letter of each book of the Bible would often be illuminated, while smaller illuminated letters would be used to emphasise particular portions of the text. Later in this book, we will examine various pages from the beautiful Winchester Bible that was produced between 1160 and 1175 (a large illuminated letter 'P' from this manuscript is shown in Figure 3).

The Romanesque style

The Romanesque period and style, which dates roughly from the late eleventh to the twelfth centuries, followed the Carolingian in the West. Although it derived its name from its attempt to recall Roman

Figure 5: 'B', Bedford Psalter and Hours.

Figure 4: A historiated initial 'B'.

principles of construction and style, it actually incorporated an international range of styles, including influences from many parts of the Western world, as well as ancient Roman, Byzantine and even Islamic styles. The late eleventh-century Carilef Bible, which is today in the care of the Dean and Chapter Library, Durham, has examples of this type of painting, in particular a large inhabited letter 'B' (Ms A11 4 folio 65). With its thin, penwork modelling and few colour washes, the construction of the letter is fairly simple, leaving much of the surface of the vellum to show through the design. The Byzantine influence can be seen in manuscripts that include hard-edged figures, heavily outlined in black, that have been adorned with damp-fold drapery (a way of depicting cloth to make it look as though it is wet and clinging to the figure).

During the tenth and eleventh centuries German scribes produced some magnificent manuscripts, while the Worms Bible, which was created in about 1148, contains a beautiful letter 'U' that commences the Old Testament Book of Hosea. Although the Italian texts that were created at this time were strongly influenced by Byzantine painting, their quality did not generally match that displayed by the texts that were produced in much of the rest of

Europe. However, there is an interesting example of an illuminated letter in the opening initial 'B' of the Camaldoli Psalter, which was made in Italy during the mid-twelfth century and can now be viewed in the British Library.

The Gothic style

By the end of the twelfth century, manuscript illustration was moving from the Romanesque to the Gothic in style, as can be seen in an early Gothic manuscript called *La Charité* Psalter (Figure 4), which was produced in France and contains an attractive letter 'B' illustrating the story of David and Goliath. A wealth of fine manuscripts, richly embellished with gold leaf, bright colours and medieval deco-

Figure 6: 'A', San Salvatore Hymnal.

ration, date from the Gothic period. Decorative borders emanating from large initial letters now became popular, leading to the production of many manuscripts whose angular Gothic-script texts were completely surrounded by detailed foliate borders full of figures, animals and birds set against richly patterned backgrounds.

Psalters, books of hours and music books

Following the foundation of universities and the general increase in literacy, the demand for books increased from the beginning of the thirteenth century, causing growing numbers of secular scribes and illuminators to emerge. In addition, the trend for religious books for public use gradually shifted towards books of a more personal nature, such as psalters. Psalters were popular, scriptural books that were used for private worship and usually contained a selection of prayers, as well as a calendar of the principal feast days. The Bedford Psalter and Hours, which was created in around 1420, is an impressive example of English illumination. About a quarter of the page is taken up by a historiated initial, while the text itself is surrounded by a border that contains scenes from the text. A letter 'B' from this psalter is illustrated here (Figure 5). Although the pages of the Bedford Psalter and Hours are large, measuring as they do 405 x 280mm (about 16 x 11"), during this period many pocket-sized bibles containing tiny illuminated initial letters were also produced, and these were regarded as valuable possessions.

The next type of book to appear was the book of hours, which

your saint, follow with accents sweet; Haste you, sad notes, fall at her flying feet: There wrapped in cloud of sorrow pity move, And tell the ravisher of my soul I perish for her love. But if she scorns my never-ceasing pain, Then burst with sighing in her sight and ne'er return again. All that I sang still to her praise did tend, Still she was first; still she my songs did end. Yet she my love and music doth both fly, The music that her echo is and beauty's sympathy; Then let my notes pursue her scornful flight: It shall suffice that they were breathed and died for her delight.

Figure 7: White-vine stem.

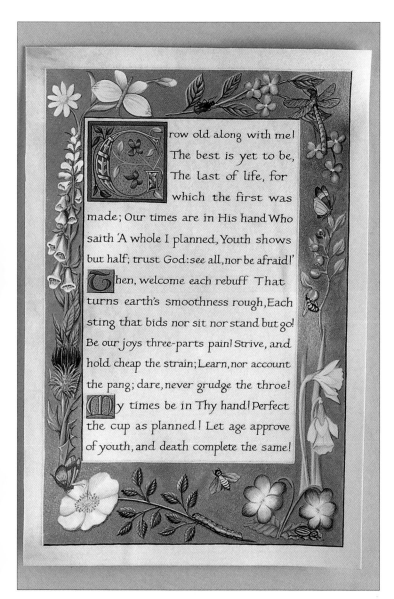

Figure 8: Trompe l'oeil.

was usually very simple, and the accompanying lettering styles were typically well adapted to the scale of the manuscripts. (We will cover music books in more detail in Chapter 7.)

The Renaissance and the advent of printing

From the mid-fourteenth century, the Renaissance, which originated in the Italian city of Florence, brought about many changes of style. As a result of scholars' attempts to emulate the classical texts of antiquity, the style of illuminated work gradually became more dense and overpowering, while the illuminated letter became less significant as detailed, naturalistic miniatures and heavy borders assumed greater prominence. White-vine-stem (Figure 7) and trompe-l'oeil borders (Figure 8) are two very attractive Renaissance styles that are particularly eye-catching, and we will cover them further in Chapter 8.

Although printing was introduced during the mid-fifteenth century, the illuminated manuscript continued to flourish, and many masterpieces were produced in the Renaissance styles in Flemish workshops during the second half of the fifteenth century. As the sixteenth century approached, the production of printed books escalated, and they therefore became more widely available. Many fine manuscripts were still being created, especially in France, Italy and Flanders, but they were now luxury items that were commissioned for special occasions, whereas printed works were becoming available to the masses. At this stage texts and outline border designs would often be printed and the colours then added to the border by hand. As printing techniques gradually became more advanced, however, the scribe and illuminator had a decreasing role to play in book production.

Inspirational illuminations

Although they are no longer created as a matter of course, we can still enjoy perusing the beautiful illuminated works of the past ten centuries. This book explores how you can spend your leisure time either recreating pages from some of these manuscripts or, by using them as your inspiration, producing new, more contemporary, designs.

Illuminated letters are very beautiful in themselves, of course, but remember to give some thought to the text that they introduce and decorate, so that you endow them with meaning. Many attractive calligraphic hands are associated with different styles of illumination, and, along with their corresponding illuminated letters, some of the principal ones are both described and used to construct the pieces in our projects. This book is not intended to be a detailed guide to calligraphy, however, and it is assumed that students will have some prior knowledge of this art form before they attempt to reproduce some of the styles illustrated.

gradually succeeded the psalter as a work of private devotion. Thousands of books of hours, whose quality and content differ greatly, survive in libraries all over the world. One of the most famous is the *Très Riches Heures* that was made for Jean, Duc de Berry, the brother of the king of France, in about 1400. This work (which you can view today in the Musée Condé at Chantilly, France) is renowned for its magnificent miniature paintings of scenes of medieval life. The artists who created them were very highly skilled, and the lettering and illumination that accompany the paintings are also of the highest quality.

Music books, for example, hymnals – large, illuminated books containing liturgical music – were often well illuminated. A fine Italian example, which was created at San Salvatore, Sienna, Italy, in 1415, includes an elaborate 'A' that orginally enclosed an illustration of the Resurrection (Figure 6). The musical notation of such hymnals

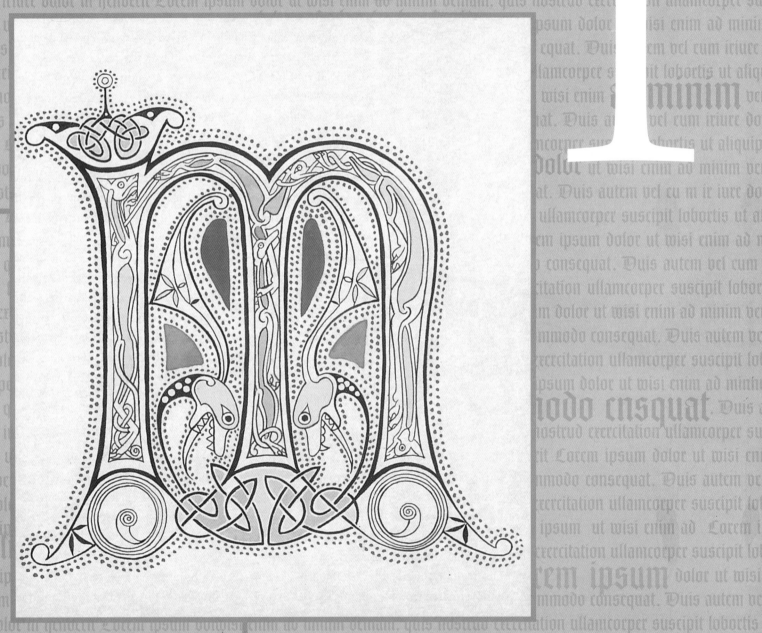

Many old manuscripts contain illuminated letters that are not completely finished, which is useful for us as students, because when we see pages in various stages of completion we can follow the construction process with ease

MATERIALS AND EQUIPMENT

In order to give your work the same durability as manuscripts whose appearance has remained unchanged over the course of centuries, you will need to use materials and methods that are as similar as possible to those that were employed when these works were produced. Although some of the methods are quite involved, and the materials expensive, because they will result in the best-quality work, it is nevertheless worth using them. You could, of course, use modern pigments, which are easy to acquire and work with and may furthermore produce works that look as good those made with the original materials, but remember that they do not have the same durability.

Writing surfaces

Vellum – calfskin – is the surface on which most illuminated manuscripts were written and painted (Figure 1). Although a few were written on paper, these are rare, and all of the examples mentioned in this book were created on vellum, which has by far the superior surface. Because vellum is expensive, however, if you are new to illumination and are unfamiliar with this surface material, you should practise on paper first and reserve vellum for your best work.

William Cowley Parchment Works is one of the few remaining manufacturers that treats and prepares skins to produce a fine, smooth, vellum surface for lettering and illumination. Various grades of vellum are made for different uses, as follows.

● **Manuscript vellum** *is the best-quality vellum. The skins are bleached of most of their natural pigment until they are a creamy-white colour. Both sides of the surface are prepared for working, which means that it can be used for books.*

● **Classic vellum** *has less of the colour bleached out of the skins than manuscript vellum, with the result that a lot of the skins' veining and yellowish-brown markings remain.*

● **Natural vellum** *retains the natural pigment of the skin and can be quite dark in colour.*

● **Binding vellum** *is used for bookbinding, but its surface has not been prepared for lettering and illumination.*

Because parchment is made from the skin of sheep, the pieces are smaller, thinner and more delicate than vellum. It is difficult to remove errors from parchment without spoiling the surface, so I therefore recommend that you use vellum instead. Although goat skin can also be written on – and, indeed, has a pleasant surface – it is usually peppered with small dots where the hairs of the animal used to be.

If you intend to begin by using paper, try to find one of good quality, such as T H Saunders or Waterford papers, which are often stocked by art shops. Ask for advice on a watercolour paper with a smooth surface that will be suitable for fine work with a pen and tiny brushes. Specialist papers and vellum can be bought by mail order.

Preparing vellum

Before it can be worked on, the surface of the vellum needs to be prepared with a powder called pounce, which is made up of powdered pumice, gum sandarac and cuttlefish. Although manuscript vellum will have been prepared with pounce before you buy it, after the piece has been cut to the required size, a final application of pounce will remove any dirt or grease and will also raise a slight nap, which will help the ink and paint to be absorbed into the skin evenly (an unpounced skin is usually too waxy to absorb ink and paint well).

Figure 1: Vellum (manuscript, classic and natural) and parchment.

Making pounce

You can buy readymade pounce or you can make it yourself. However, making your own is not only easy, but you will be sure of having mixed the ingredients for your particular requirements correctly. Powdered pumice and gum sandarac are available, while dry cuttlefish can be bought from pet shops.

Pigments

The pigments that were used by early scribes were coloured substances (Figure 4) that were mixed with water and egg yolk or gum to bind them together. Organic pigments were obtained from plants or animals, while mineral pigments came the earth or were manmade substances.

The chief requisites of a pigment are, firstly, that it should have a strong, brilliant hue that has no impurities, secondly, that it will not fade when exposed to sunlight for long periods, thirdly, that it does not become discoloured and, finally, that is capable of being made into a smooth, finely ground fluid that can be applied to the writing surface with great accuracy. Many of today's pigments contain acids that will cause discolouration over time, a consideration that you will need to bear in mind if you want to produce work that will still look as fresh as when you created it after many years. Artists' Colourmen produce finely ground pigments that you can buy in the quantity that you require, however small. A wide range of colours is available, of which the most suitable for illumination are given below.

Making pounce

Figure 2: Pestle, mortar and pounce ingredients (powdered pumice, cuttlefish, gum sandarac crystals).

| Use a pestle and mortar – available from cookery shops – to grind up the powdered pumice, gum sandarac and cuttlefish into a very fine powder (Figure 2). Roughly equal proportions of each ingredient should be used, so grind up one or two cuttlefish and then measure out the other ingredients in matching proportions and grind them together well. You will need about a level tablespoon to a square foot (about 30.5cm²) of vellum.

2 When the ingredients have been ground together to make a very fine powder, shake the mortar from side to side. Remove the larger particles that come to the surface, which could scratch the vellum if you rub in the pounce too hard. You can store the prepared pounce in a clean jar (covered with a lid) and keep it indefinitely – any left-over pounce can similarly be saved for future use.

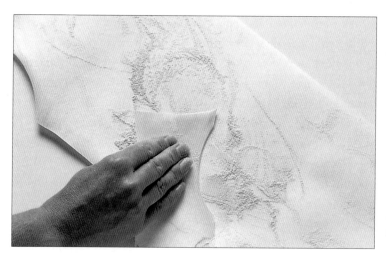

Fig.ure 3: Pouncing vellum.

3 To prepare the vellum for writing or painting, first sprinkle the pounce over the surface as shown in Figure 3. Using a small offcut of vellum, work the powder into the skin using steady, circular movements. You will need to apply a reasonable amount of pressure so that you remove any dirt and grease and raise a slight velvety nap on the vellum, but be careful not to mark the surface. Most skins will require about 8 to 10 minutes of rubbing. As you are rubbing, watch the surface carefully, and if you think that you may be damaging it, stop. Most vellum can take quite a lot of pouncing, but it is important that you do not raise too much of a nap, which will make writing or painting fine lines difficult.

4 When you have finished, return any excess pounce to the storage jar and then dust off the skin. Hold it up by one corner and flick the surface lightly with a tissue so that the texture is not disturbed but a minimal dusting of powder remains. The vellum is now ready for use.

● **BLUE:** the two blue pigments that were chiefly used in medieval times were genuine ultramarine (ground and purified lapis lazuli) and azurite (a copper carbonate). These are very difficult to obtain, but artificial or French ultramarine is a good substitute. Although it contains sulphur, which may become discoloured in the presence of acid, this can be avoided with care. Cerulean blue is a strong, permanent colour, while cobalt blue (which is also permanent) is paler than ultramarine, but capable of producing good results.

● **RED:** vermilion has been used for over a thousand years and still remains the illuminator's principal colour. A compound of mercury and sulphur, it possesses all of the required characteristics of a good pigment: permanence, opacity and a smooth texture. Scarlet vermilion produces the shade of red that can be seen on most early manuscripts.

● **GREEN:** viridian (emerald oxide of chromium) is the best shade of green to use. Although it is both permanent and brilliant in hue, it requires the addition of an opaque pigment, such as lemon yellow or Chinese white, to remove its transparency. The medieval scribes used malachite – a basic carbonate of copper – which was a beautiful colour. The cost of its preparation has made it very difficult to obtain today, however.

● **YELLOW:** lemon yellow has both a good consistency and a bright colour. Note that chrome yellows are made from lead, which will blacken with age. Although it is a permanent colour, yellow ochre (an earth pigment) is rather dull for use in illumination.

● **BROWN:** burnt sienna and umber are the earth pigments that artists most commonly use. Although they are rather heavy and dull, and can also be difficult to apply with a really fine touch, as with other earth pigments the colours are permanent.

● **BLACK:** lamp black and ivory black are charcoal-based pigments that are suitable for illumination. They are derived from the carbon in burnt materials, such as bones and oil.

● **WHITE:** Chinese, or zinc, white is a smooth-textured and permanent pigment that will not darken with age. Do not use flake white, however, because this contains lead and will turn brown when exposed to sulphur.

Figure 4: Powdered pigments (ultramarine, vermilion, zinc white, lamp black, viridian, lemon yellow and burnt sienna).

Mixing media

The easiest pigments to use are those that have been bound together with gum in cake form, which only have to be mixed with water before use. Because one of the main charms of illuminated work is its brilliance, it is important to keep your colours as clean as possible. Remember that it is all too easy to make a pigment dull by mixing it with impure water or using dirty brushes, so take care to avoid contaminating your pigments. Tap water contains many undesirable chemicals as regards illumination, so try to use distilled water, which is readily obtained from chemists, as you progress. You should also eventually aim to use powdered pigments, as well as making your own binding media, all of which will produce stronger, brighter colours.

The preparation of three types of binding media – gum water, egg whites and egg yolks – that were used in medieval times are described below. Although each takes some time to prepare, they will all produce the long-lasting results that were achieved in medieval manuscripts.

Making binding media

1 To make gum water, first mix one part gum-arabic crystals to two parts distilled water and leave the mixture to dissolve overnight. The next day, strain the liquid through a piece of muslin. The resulting mixture can be kept in a glass jar for use as and when you need it.

2 To begin with, dilute the mixture with an equal proportion of water to make the required strength. You will soon learn which pigments require a stronger or weaker solution of gum water. If you use too much gum, the colour may either crack when it is dry, or, if you are using it with a pen, the paint may not flow smoothly. If you use too little gum, the pigment may not be fixed to the page firmly enough. Always test the colour on a scrap of paper or vellum to see what happens when it dries. Try rubbing the pigment with your finger to make sure that it is firmly fixed to the page. Remember that you can easily make adjustments at this stage, and that it is very discouraging when you have spent a great deal of time painting areas of colour only to find that problems later occur.

3 Egg white is used to make glair, or clarea, a binding medium of early medieval times. First separate the white of an egg from the yolk and beat the white thoroughly in a shallow bowl until it is stiff enough to remain in the bowl when you turn the bowl upside down. (This step is vital if you want the eventual fluid to have the correct texture.) Tilt the bowl slightly and leave it overnight.

4 The following day, pour the distilled liquid (which should have run to the bottom of the bowl) into a jar. The liquid will only keep for a few days, after which it will thicken and dry up. Mix the glair with the pigment and a little distilled water until you have obtained the consistency that you require.

5 Egg yolk can also be used as a binding agent. First, separate the yolk from the white, making sure that the yolk remains intact. Carefully lift and then break the yolk into a container, so that the liquid runs out of the yolk's skin into the bowl. Add a roughly equal quantity of water to the yolk, but remember that the exact proportions required can vary slightly from colour to colour, as you will learn with practice.

6 Mix the egg-yolk liquid with powdered pigment until its consistency resembles thin cream. You will find that the yolk's yellow colour disappears from the pigment, which becomes very hard when it has dried.

7 If you find that you have problems with paint that has not adhered sufficiently to the page, you can paint over these parts with a weak version of any of these binding agents. Make sure that you do not use too strong a mixture, however, because this could give an unpleasant gloss to your work.

PROJECT: *Applying colours*

Each style of illumination is given unique distinction by the combination of colours used. The medieval monk's palette did not incorporate the range that is available to us today, and a deep, vibrant blue, an almost terracotta-hued shade of red and a green the colour of lead roofs are the colours that immediately spring to mind as being characteristic of medieval illumination.

The letter illustrated in Figure 5 is taken from a late-thirteenth-century Italian manuscript and uses ultramarine blue and vermilion red, plus a popular shade of pale pink that was obtained by mixing white with a little vermilion. We will begin by making this simply decorated letter.

Figure 5: The finished letter.

Brushes, pens and inks

You will need very fine brushes made from sable fur to produce the precise detail that is required for illuminated work, and most art shops stock brushes of this quality. A size 0 or 1 is small enough for the finest details, while a slightly larger brush can be used for painting large areas of colour. In order not to spoil your sable brushes, use larger-sized brushes of a less good quality to mix your pigments.

Because quill pens – the favoured writing instruments of the Middle Ages – produce very fine, delicate strokes, you should use one for writing the text if you can (art shops or specialist outlets sometimes stock them). Otherwise, use a pen with a square-cut, metal nib that has been specifically manufactured for calligraphy. I recommend William Mitchell's Round-Hand series nibs, which range in size from 0, the largest, to 6, the smallest (there are 12 nib sizes in total, including half sizes).

The inks that were used by medieval scribes were made either from oak gall nuts or from the carbon obtained from lamp black. Many modern bottled inks are not permanent, so you should ideally use Chinese stick ink, which is ground with water in an ink slate, instead.

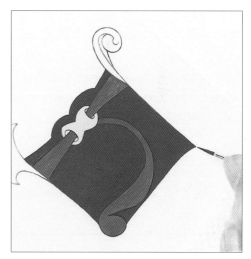

1 Draw a very faint outline of the letter on the page. Mix the powdered pigments with your chosen medium of either glair, egg yolk or gum water and some distilled water. Use either a ceramic palette that has a lid or a small, deep container, such as an egg cup, which will prevent the paint from drying out too quickly.

2 Apply the paint with a small sable brush to give a smooth, even covering on which you can later paint detail if you want. This opaque covering of paint can be seen on most early manuscripts, especially in the case of the more dominant colours. Although some of the secondary colours, which required more preparation and were not used with such regularity, were often applied with less precision, the better-quality manuscripts maintained a solid, opaque covering. This is what you should try to achieve on all of your letters, whether they are quite small and simple, like this one, or will later be given further layers of detail and special treatments.

3 In order to give it precision and crispness, outline the letter in a darker colour. Some medieval artists outlined the original drawing in ink and then painted in the base colours. This method can be advantageous for some pieces, particularly Celtic work, which frequently requires many intricate outlines to be drawn, but virtually no subsequent detail to be added. If you decide on this method, remember that you will often have to retouch and redefine the outline after you have added the colours.

THE USE OF GOLD

If gilding is required, this must be done before any of the paint is applied. Gold forms such an integral part of most illuminated work that we will cover the various methods of application in some detail.

There are basically three types of real gold that can be used for illumination: gold powder, transfer gold leaf and loose gold leaf (Figure 6). Although various metallic-gold paints are also available today, which may initially appear very effective, in a side-by-side comparison they cannot compete with the brilliance and depth of colour of real gold (Figure 7).

After gold has been applied, it is polished, or burnished, to give it as bright a shine as possible. You will therefore need burnishing tools, and there are three types of burnisher that you will find useful at various stages: dog-tooth, flat and pencil burnishers (Figure 8). You will also need a pair of sharp scissors that you should use exclusively for cutting sheets of gold, as well as a soft brush for removing excess gold.

Figure 6: Gold powder, loose leaf and transfer leaf.

Figure 7: Types of gold for illumination – imitation gold paint, gold powder, flat transfer gold leaf, raised loose gold leaf.

Gold powder

Illuminating gold, which usually measures 23 carats and comes in powdered form, is available in 1g quantities. Although this equates to only half a teaspoon of powder, it goes quite a long way. It can be purchased in small pots. These little pots, or another small, deep container with a lid, such as a 35mm-film container, can be used for mixing the gold with distilled water and liquid gum arabic to create the correct consistency for painting (gum arabic is sold in small bottles by most art shops).

When working with gold, it is important that you keep your materials as clean as possible. Ordinary tap water contains too many chemicals to be used with gold, because the purer the gold the brighter its brilliance.

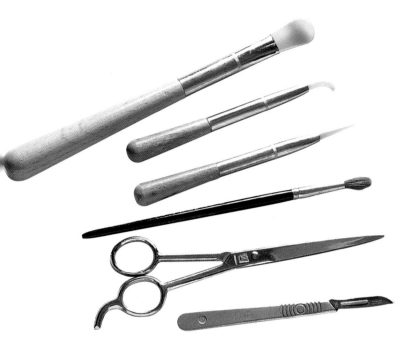

Figure 8: Burnishing tools (Flat, dog-tooth and pencil burnishers, scissors and soft brush).

Wash any brushes that you use for painting with gold in a pot of distilled water and keep the brushes separate from those that you use with paint. Although you can also use a pen to write with gold powder, the gold particles tend to separate from the liquid so quickly that you will painstakingly have to remix and refill your brush with the correct mixture after every few strokes.

Working with powdered gold

You will need only one or two small drops of gum arabic per 1g of gold powder. Dip a small paintbrush into the bottle of gum arabic and let a drop fall into the gold powder, then repeat the process with a second drop. About half a teaspoon of water is all that is required, so use a measuring spoon until you get used to judging the quantities by sight. Using a paintbrush that you have reserved for working in gold, mix the water with the gold powder until all of the gold particles have dispersed throughout the liquid. Note that the gold powder will gradually separate from the liquid and that it will therefore have to remixed at intervals while you are working.

Check that the consistency is correct by painting a small test area – about 1cm ($^7/_{16}$") square – with the gold powder. Give it about 15 minutes to dry. Then, using a dog-tooth burnisher, polish the surface gently, until it has become smooth and has a good shine (figure 9). If the gold sticks to the burnisher, it is probably not dry, so leave it a little longer. If it flakes away from the surface, there is not enough gum arabic in the mixture. On the other hand, if the burnisher makes dark streaks on the gold, there is too much gum arabic in the

mixture. It is easier to add more gum arabic than to remove it from the mixture, so err on the side of caution when you are mixing the gum arabic with the gold powder, as you can easily add more later.

Loose gold leaf

Loose gold leaf is purchased in books of 25 sheets that are the same size as sheets of transfer gold leaf. Two thicknesses – single and double – are available, and you will need a book of each in order to achieve the best results.

The loose gold leaf should be applied over gesso, a thin plaster base. Although a few outlets sell readymade gesso, it is better to make your own.

Although creating raised gilding with loose gold leaf is a painstaking process, the results are spectacular, and if you manage to apply the gold leaf successfully you will be rewarded with a real sense of achievement.

Figure 9: Test piece of gold powder, half burnished.

PROJECT: *Making and using gesso*

INGREDIENTS

8 parts slaked white plaster of Paris

3 parts white lead

1 part preserving sugar

1 part Seccotine glue

A pinch Armenian bole

Distilled water

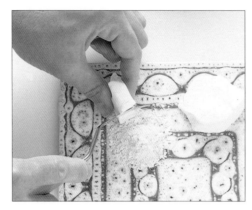

1 Grate the plaster to a rough powder by grinding the edge with a palette knife.

2 Measure the correct amount into the mortar using a small measuring spoon.

3 Add white lead, levelling off the spoonful carefully with a palette knife before adding it to the mortar.

4 Add a spoonful of finely ground preserving sugar (grind it with a pestle).

5 Add a level spoonful of glue.

6 Add a pinch of Armenian bole. The point of the palette knife can be used to pick up the small quantity required.

7 Add distilled water, taking great care to allow only a few drops at a time to drip from the container.

8 Grind the gesso ingredients to the consistency of treacle. It is very important that the ingredients are both completely mixed and finely ground. Pour the gesso on to a piece of aluminium foil, making a small, circular shape. Leave it to dry overnight.

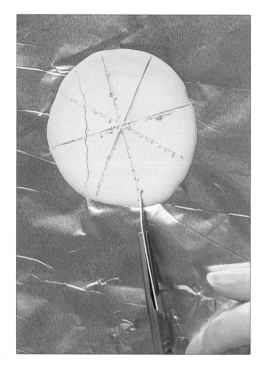

9 Cut the gesso into diagonal segments. It is vital that you cut it in the manner shown because the ingredients will have separated slightly, some moving to the inside and others to the outside of the pool of gesso, and this method of cutting will therefore ensure that there is an even quantity of ingredients in each portion.

10 When you are ready to use a piece of gesso, peel a segment away from the foil, touching it as little as possible. Break it up into small pieces in a mixing palette or egg cup. Add about half a teaspoon of water, so that the water surrounds all of the pieces. Leave the gesso to soak for about half an hour.

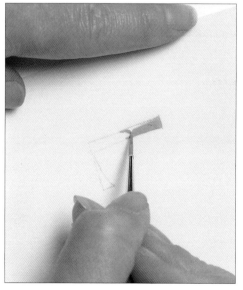

11 You will have to mix the gesso very carefully so that you don't introduce any air bubbles. Using the end of a paintbrush, stir the gesso slowly and carefully, until all of the pieces have dissolved and the mixture is smooth, with a consistency resembling single cream.

12 The gesso can now painted on to the areas of the work that will be gilded. Work on a flat surface, so that the gesso does not run down to the bottom of the letter. Using a small brush, paint on a thin layer of gesso, taking care to keep it smooth and even. Now leave it to dry overnight.

PROJECT: *Using gold leaf*

When the gesso is dry, you can apply a layer of single-thickness loose gold leaf. Note that because it is so thin and fragile, loose gold leaf is quite difficult to cut. Using a pair of scissors that you have reserved exclusively for this purpose, first cut a piece of loose gold leaf to roughly the size required, cutting through the backing paper, too. When large areas are to be gilded, work over the gesso using squares of gold no larger than 2.5cm (1") square, applying them piece by piece until the whole area is covered. Then brush away the excess gold.

1 Holding the book of loose gold leaf open as shown, make a decisive cut of the length needed.

2 Now make the second cut, letting the piece of gold leaf and its backing paper slip onto the work surface. Now close the book of gold leaf and put it down, away from your immediate work area, so that you do not disturb it as you work.

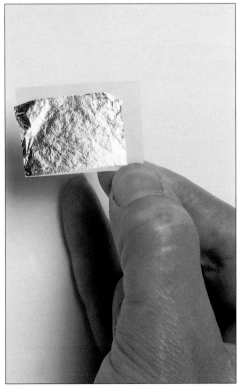

3 Pick up the square of gold leaf that you have cut by a corner, so that you are holding only a tiny portion of it before you apply it.

4 The gesso must now be moistened in the same way as gold size (see page 24), that is, by breathing on it several times. Start with ten breaths. As soon as you have finished the tenth breath, place the gold leaf over the gesso, with the backing paper facing upwards.

5 With a dog-tooth burnisher, smooth the gold on to the gesso by rubbing over the backing paper. Use light, circular motions, so that the gesso is not dented while it is in its softened state.

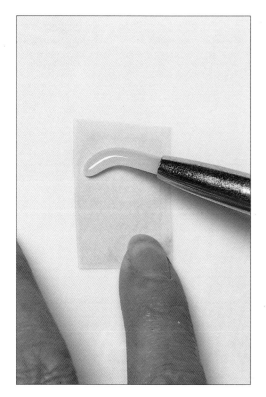

6 Remove the backing paper and burnish the gold itself with the dog-tooth burnisher. If it has stuck to the gesso successfully, you should be able to polish it to a beautiful shine.

7 With a pencil burnisher, carefully work around the edges of the gesso to make sure that the gold has adhered to these parts.

8 Using a soft brush, brush away the excess gold around the edges. If necessary, you could now apply another layer of single-thickness loose gold leaf to any areas that have not been fully covered. Because the gesso will have retained some its dampness, any subsequent layers will require fewer breaths than the first.

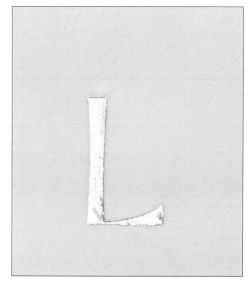

9 Here is the finished letter, with the whole of the gesso covered with two layers of gold leaf.

PROJECT: *Working with transfer gold leaf*

Transfer gold leaf can be purchased in small sheets about 10cm (around 4") square, and in books of 25 leaves. It is fairly easy to apply, and gold size, a strong-smelling, yellow liquid made with ammonia, is the medium that you should use.

3 Then smooth over the areas of the letter that will be gilded with a dog-tooth burnisher. You should start to see an impression where the gold has stuck to the size.

1 Paint the gold size on to the area that will be gilded and then let it dry. Work on a flat surface, so that the size lies in an even layer on the page. When it is dry, moisten it slightly by breathing on it until it becomes adhesive. Breathe on the size as if you were breathing on a mirror, and do not touch it with your lips. The number of breaths that you will need to use varies, depending on the weather conditions. If you are working on a hot, dry, summer's day, for example, as many as fifteen breaths may be needed, while in cool, damp conditions only four or five may be required.

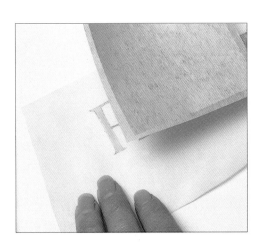

2 Transfer gold leaf is very forgiving, and you can apply and reapply it to the surface until all of the size has been covered. Lay a sheet of transfer gold, gold side down, over the dampened size.

4 Take away the sheet when you think that the gold has attached itself to the letter. If it has done so successfully, you should see a perfect, negative impression of your letter on the gold sheet. If one or two areas of the gold size are not fully covered, breathe on the work again and reapply a fresh section of gold from the sheet. Because gold blends into itself, you should be able to eradicate any overlapping edges. Using a soft brush, lightly brush away any excess gold that has adhered to the vellum.

iriure dolor in henderit ut wisi enim ad minim , quis nostrud exercitation
ncorper suscipit lobortis ut aliquip ex ea commodo consequat. Duis autem vel cum iriure dolor in henderit Lorem ipsum
isi enim ad minim veniam, quis nostrud exercitation ullamcorper suscipit lobortis ut ali quip ex ea commodo consequat.
m vel cum iriure dolor in henderit Lorem ipsum dolor ut wisi enim ad minim veniam, quis nostrud exercitation ullamco
cipit lobortis ut aliquiperea commodo consequat. Duis autem vel cum iriure dolor in Lorem ipsum
enim ad minim veniam, quis nostrud exercitation ullamcorper suscipit lobortis ut ali consequat.

Chapter 2

Having learnt the basic application methods for colours and gold, we shall now move on to making use of them on specific styles of letter, starting with Celtic lettering.

CELTIC LETTERING AND ILLUMINATION

Figure 1: Celtic letters used for large initials.

The origins of the very distinctive Celtic lettering and illumination lie in the finely decorated religious books that were produced in Ireland and the north and west of England and Scotland during the sixth to ninth centuries. The finest, as well as the best-known, example is the Book of Kells, which is housed in Trinity College, Dublin, Ireland (see page 7, Figure 1), whose lettering is so detailed and intricate that it is quite stunning to behold, even though the years have dulled the brilliance of some of the colours. Different pages are displayed from time to time, and although some very good books contain excellent reproductions of the manuscript, they can't compare with the original. Standing in front of the Book of Kells, you can picture the monks at work, laboriously painting the tiny details day by day, using carefully prepared pigments and writing tools.

The text of most Celtic manuscripts is in Latin. The shape of the illuminated letters varied from artist to artist, but the general shape and style of the letters of the alphabet shown in Figure 1 are a good starting point and will match the decoration that we will cover later in the chapter. Because some of the letters, such as the 'K', were not part of the Latin alphabet, these have been formed in the same style as the others.

PROJECT: *An illuminated 'U'*

We shall first construct a simply illuminated 'U'. The example shown in Figure 2 formed part of the Latin word *uae*. The letter 'A' sits inside the 'U', and the 'E' followed on in uncial script (uncial script will be explained further later in the chapter).

Letters of this degree of complexity were often written for the initial letter of each paragraph down the left-hand border of a page, so there could be four to ten illuminated letters on a page. The height of the letters was usually between 2 and 4cm ($^{13}/_{16}$ and 1 $^{9}/_{16}$"). Larger, more detailed, Celtic letters were made up of a complex collection of patterns that were pieced together to form the required letter shape. The various types of pattern used are discussed below.

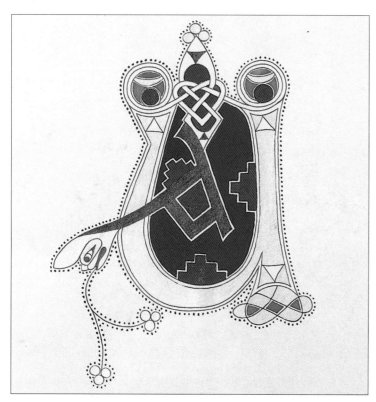

Figure 2: Illuminated 'U' from a Book of Kells' original.

1 Make a drawing of the letter on either thin layout paper or tracing paper. If you need to position the drawing so that it matches up with other parts of a piece of work, it will help if you use tracing paper, because you can see exactly where you are placing the design. You will need to use a very hard, sharp pencil when you are making the drawing, however, as tracing paper tends to blunt pencils very quickly.

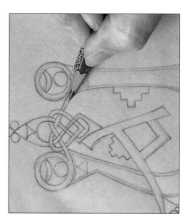

2 Trace the drawing onto your piece of vellum or paper using red transfer paper or else trace over the back of the design and then trace down the lines from the front again, which is a more painstaking process.

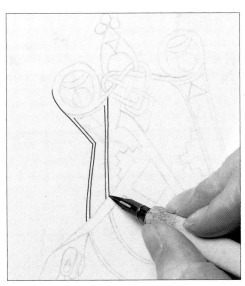

3 Red transfer paper can be made by rubbing some Armenian bole or burnt sienna pigment into greaseproof paper or tracing paper. The only parts that need not be traced down and outlined at this stage are any details that will be painted over the top of other colours, which you should trace into place after the base colour has been painted. There are no areas of this sort in the 'U', but the 'T' shown later in the chapter has detailing on the head of the animal that was not included in the first tracing of the design because it was necessary to paint in the cream-coloured background first.

4 Outline the whole letter using ink and a fine mapping pen. You will be able to see where the design needs sharpening up – some lines can be rather blurred or uneven after having been traced into place. Smoother, rounded curves can be given to all of the lines, and you can now fill in any parts of the design that were not transferred from the tracing properly. You should end up with a complete line drawing of the image. Note that you will need a steady hand on some areas where the lines are extremely thin and curved.

5 When you have finished inking the outline, rub out any surplus red transfer powder, or graphite powder from the pencil, to leave a strong, clear image that has no blurred or incomplete areas. The next step is to apply a gold colour to the designated areas. No gold was used in the Book of Kells, the material used instead being orpiment (arsenic trisulphide), which had a bright, shiny appearance. If orpiment is placed alongside other pigments, however, it will discolour them, a fact of which the illuminators of the Book of Kells were well aware. In order to prevent the orpiment coming into contact with the other pigments, they therefore either painted a border of ink around gold-coloured areas or else left a thin margin of blank vellum between the gold colouring and other pigments. You could use one of a variety of gold paints or gold powder, which is a good medium for this sort of design.

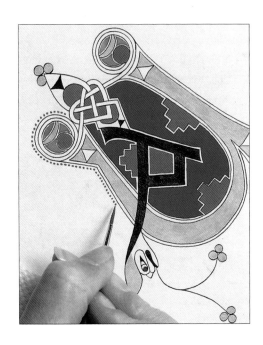

6 LEFT Winsor and Newton's gold gouache was used for the example shown. Take care to overlap the outlines as little as possible when applying the gold, because although you can go over the outlines again to neaten the letter at a later stage, it is not easy to cover over gold leaf because it will resist ink.

7 RIGHT To complete the letter, now add the colours. Note that many of the inner parts of the letter have not been coloured, which means that the surface of the vellum can be seen. Very little modelling (the use of light and dark shades of colour to give the effect of three-dimensional shapes) was used in Celtic illumination. Various effects were instead created by using different textures and weights of line or patterning, as well as changes of colour.

PROJECT: *Making a knotwork pattern*

Knotwork patterns are complex, interwoven pieces of decoration that should consist of a single, continuous line that weaves under and over itself in a carefully designed pattern. They have to be constructed with precision, so that each piece of the pattern weaves in and out correctly. An easy way to see how this works is to practise the following method.

Decide on a simple, linear pattern to make into a piece of knotwork and sketch it lightly. When you are drawing the pattern, take care not to make any areas too small to outline (Figure 3) – a little trial and error will soon teach you which patterns to avoid.

Outline the shapes that have been made where the lines cross, and also draw an outline around the outside of the shape.

Next, working around the pattern, connect the outlined areas with heavier lines, or perhaps a coloured pencil, until the whole pattern has been constructed with under- and over-bridges. This example only needed two crossovers, but more detailed designs will need dozens. If you ensure that you always alternate under- and over-pieces, the pattern should work out correctly. When you are drawing the outlines, remember to go around every part of the pattern, because if you leave one piece out the crossovers will not work correctly. When the middle line is removed you can see the effect of the woven pattern.

Strips of knotwork

Strips of knotwork are often needed for illuminating letters, and you should start by drawing a guideline consisting of a row of dots. Figure 5 illustrates a simple plait that has been formed by one row of dots spaced at equal intervals.

Make a row of dots as illustrated in Figure 5, and then link every other dot with a pencilled arch, as shown.

Next, draw in the outline pieces that have been made by the crossing lines in each section, as well as around the outer edges.

Now work on the crossovers so that you form a continuous, weaving line. When you have finished the pattern, trace the lines that you

Figure 3:
a Make a simple linear pattern to form the basis of a piece of knotwork.

b Outline each part.

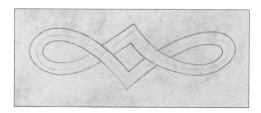

c Form bridges where each line crosses.

d The finished pattern.

Figure 4: Avoid patterns with areas which are too small to be outlined properly.

Figure 5: A simple knotwork plait formed from a row of dots.

Figure 6: A plait formed from two rows of dots.

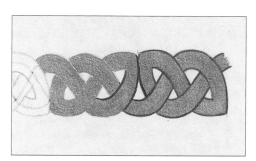

Figure 7: Vary the pattern by breaking and rejoining the line at different points.

Figure 8: Three rows of dots and several breaks are used to create this pattern.

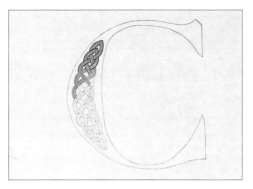

Figure 9: Fit knotwork into irregular shapes around a pattern of dots. The ends of the knotwork need to be carefully worked to fill the area fully.

Figure 10: Knotwork pattern used for the letter 'T' on page 39.

require for your work so that you lose the guideline dots and arches that helped you to form the pattern and use the tracing instead.

Figure 6 shows a plait pattern that was formed in the same manner, but from two rows of dots.

In Figure 7 a variation has been added to the plait by turning the weaving line back on itself at intervals. This is done by breaking two of the lines and joining each broken end to a new partner, so that the weave continues correctly. In order to turn the direction of the weave where you decide to break the lines in a pattern, make sure that you round off both broken ends and reconnect them with the correct new pieces.

Figure 8 shows a pattern based on three rows of dots. The weaving lines have been broken and reconnected in several places to form an interesting effect.

In order to fit a knotwork pattern into a letter's outline, you will first need to draw the area that will be filled with the pattern and then, working by eye, add rows of dots until you have filled it (Figure 9). Follow the procedure of linking the dots together, then drawing the outline pieces and so on. The ends of pointed areas should be carefully worked so that the pattern fits the shape neatly, but without breaking the continuously weaving line.

More complex patterns can also be made, and figures 10–12 illustrate the construction of a few others, broken down into stages. Figure 10 shows the knotwork pattern that was used for the letter 'T' later in the chapter. Although the pattern is straightforward around the thicker parts of the letter, it was too wide for the whole area along the thinner strip at the top, so it was worked into a simpler design at either end. Note how the artist carefully linked the two parts of the letter.

In order to join two different knotwork patterns, you will have to break them both off at a suitable point and then link the broken ends of each pattern. For now, you will only need to make one break in each pattern (Figure 13). When you become more skilled, however, you can work out really complex connections that link different patterns in several places.

When joining two different pieces of knotwork, if you find that you have two under-crosses to connect and two over-crosses that would not form the correct sequence, you will have to flip one of the patterns over to make the lines join correctly. If the reversed image is not the correct shape, you will have to rework the design. Make sure that the new design has lines that follow the reversed pattern direction, so that the broken ends join the other piece of knotwork correctly.

Figure 11: Looped pattern.

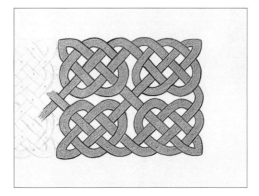

Figure 12: Box-shaped pattern.

Figure 13: Joining together two different pieces of knotwork requires careful planning.

SPIRAL PATTERNS

Spiral patterns were used a great deal in insular decoration, and some great manuscripts contain extremely complicated patterns consisting of whole panels of interlocking spirals. Although these pages can look dauntingly complex, the individual spirals are actually quite simple to draw – it's just a matter of learning some of the basic designs, as well as how they are linked. You can then work up a pattern that links as many spirals as you need to fill the available space in, or around, a letter.

The construction of the simplest forms of spiral are shown in figures 14-16. A one-coil spiral starts either from the centre point or from a small, central circle. Two- and three-coil spirals enable you to interweave different colours (figures 17-18). Variations can then be given to the centres of the spirals in the form of smaller circles that turn back on themselves (figures 19–20), with tiny, pointed ovals being used to separate areas of colour (Figure 21) within each spiral.

Joining the spirals creates further large areas, which are frequently subdivided by three pointed shapes (Figure 22). (Remember that neither the spirals nor their surrounding shapes have to form a balanced, repeating pattern.) You can gradually build up an intricate piece of pattern constructed of spirals and joining filler shapes to fit any area that you want to decorate. The space in the centre of the 'O' shown in Figure 23 has been filled with spirals in this manner.

Figure 14: One-coil spiral from centre point.

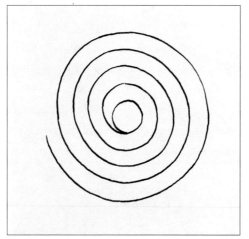

Figure 15: One-coil spiral from central circle.

Figure 16: A variation on a one-coil spiral.

Figure 17: A two-coil spiral.

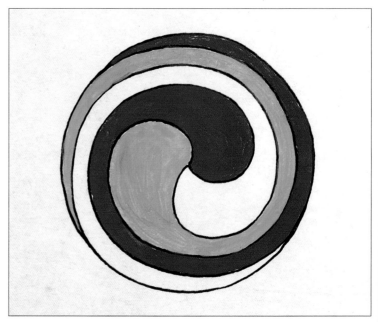

Figure 18: A three-coil spiral.

Figure 19: Varying the centres of spirals with inner coils.

Figure 20: Three central spirals are used in this pattern.

Figure 21: Pointed ovals used to separate areas within spirals.

Figure 22. Joining spirals together is very simple.

Figure 23: A letter 'O' with a spiral-filled centre.

KEY PATTERNS

Key patterns are another distinctive feature of Celtic illumination that often form either part of a large, illuminated letter or a carpet page of intricate design. The use of linear patterns of this sort dates from ancient times, and the insular artists made use of a complex array of patterns with which to adorn their manuscripts.

To begin with, you will need to use a grid of small squares to form the interlocking patterns (a few simple ones are shown in figures 24–26). Borders can be made of strips of pattern (Figure 27). Having devised a colour scheme, you can strengthen the pattern after you have painted in the colours by reinforcing the partition lines with dark outlines (figures 28–29).

Figure 24. Simple key patterns – 1.

Figure 25: Simple key patterns – 2.

Figure 26: Simple key patterns – 3.

Figure 27: Key-pattern borders.

Figure 28: Key-pattern colour schemes – 1.

Figure 29: Key-pattern colour schemes – 2.

Once you have mastered the basics, you can create more complex designs, filling in areas of solid colour to break up the monotony of large areas of tiny squares (figures 30–31). The strips of pattern can be made to curve around other shapes (Figure 32), as well as to fit into specific areas (Figure 33). They can be intermixed with knotwork to good effect, too (Figure 34).

Figure 30: Sketch the pattern.

Figure 31: Paint in the colours and outlines.

Figure 32: Curved key patterns.

Figure 33: Irregular shapes.

Figure 34: Knotwork and key patterns together.

ZOOMORPHICS AND ANTHROPOMORPHICS

Celtic work is full of delightful little birds, animals and human figures that intertwine with letters and fill gaps between paragraphs. The animal and bird patterns are known as zoomorphics, while those using the human figure are called anthropomorphics. Figure 35 shows a small bird that appears in the middle of a large block of text and acts as a letter 'Q', while the dog-like animal pictured in Figure 36 also appears within the body of the text on a page, preceded by a large and elaborate capital letter. The heads of all of the Celtic animals and birds are constructed similarly (Figure 37), with a long mouth coloured differently from the neck and body, a small, round eye and an oval-shaped head leading into the neck. Repeating patterns – of birds in particular – are used to form borders and large areas of pattern within letters (Figure 38). Panels of each of the forms of pattern mentioned in the last two pages can be linked to form larger letters with bands of different colours (Figure 41). These bands can in turn be worked into animal heads and bodies, further linking the letters or bringing them to interesting terminations (Figure 42).

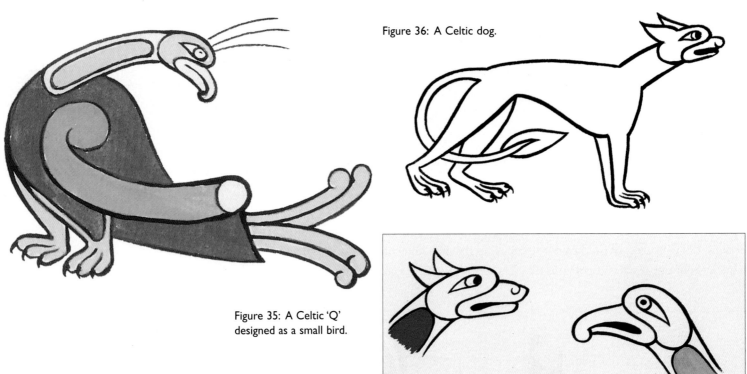

Figure 36: A Celtic dog.

Figure 35: A Celtic 'Q' designed as a small bird.

Figure 37: Heads of animals and birds.

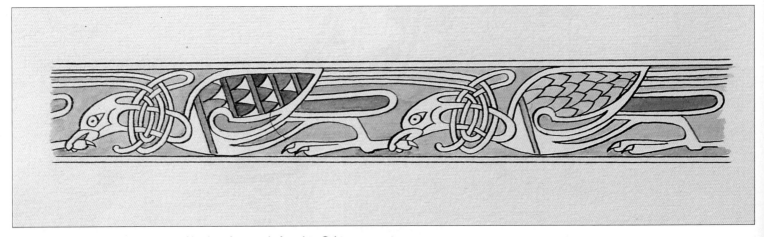

Figure 38: A repeat border pattern of birds is frequently found in Celtic manuscripts.

The human forms are also very stylised. A beautiful portrait of St John appears in the centre of folio 291v of the Book of Kells, illustrating the typically formal, curling arrangement of the hair and the simple facial details (Figure 39). Slightly more crudely constructed faces – always sharing the same basic, pen-formed design – were often slipped into any available space within a letter (Figure 40).

Figure 39: A portrait of St John from the Book of Kells.

Figure 40: Simpler, cruder faces are often used.

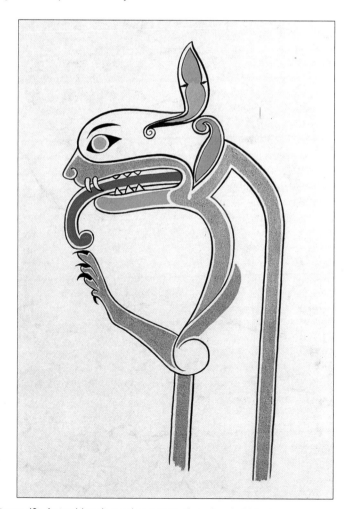

Figure 42: Animal heads used as terminals to banded blocks.

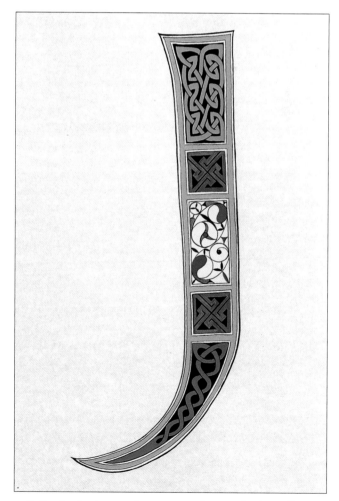

Figure 41: Bands of colour enclose patterns, forming this letter 'J'.

PROJECT: *Creating a Celtic initial letter 'H'*

We will now reproduce a large, initial letter 'H' (Figure 43), which begins a long strip of lettering that reads *Hic est Iohannis* ('Here is John') (Figure 50). The second letter, an 'I', sits inside the 'H'. The remaining letters accompanying the initial are written in the heavy, angular style that often preceded the main body of the text on the illuminated section of a page. A full alphabet of these letters is shown below.

1 Trace the outline of the 'H'. The original knotwork pattern is quite complex, so this version has been slightly simplified. As you draw the interwoven portions, make sure that each piece weaves in and out correctly, following regularly over and under without missing a crossing point.

Figure 43: An initial letter 'H'.

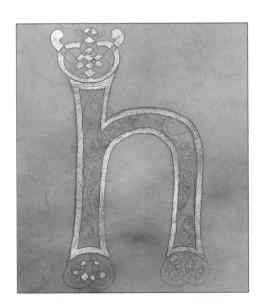

2 Apply the gold work to the outer borders.

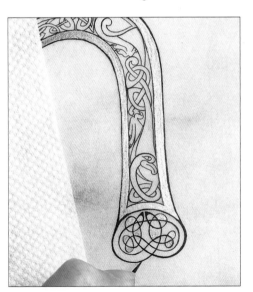

3 Now outline the whole of the letter.

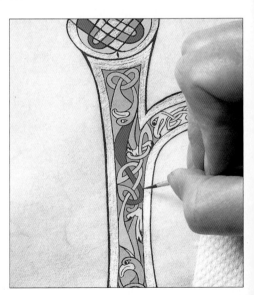

4 Apply the colours to complete the letter. If necessary, go over any parts of the outline that were lost when you added the colours so that the image is sharp and clear.

PROJECT: *Creating a title strip*

I If you wish to continue writing the title strip that was begun with the letter 'H', make a drawing of the 'I' within the 'H' (see step 1, page 36) and the remaining letters. Trace these into place on the vellum (see step 1, page 36), then add the gold, followed by the colours.

An alphabet of angulated capital letters is shown in Figure 44. These are used for the remaining letters of the title strip.

Figure 50: The completed title strip

WRITING AND ILLUMINATING UNCIAL LETTERS

The script that makes up the body of the text in Celtic manuscripts is called uncial. In order to write uncial letters, you will have to hold your pen at a much shallower angle (about 30°) than for most of the later scripts. Practise holding the pen at this angle by writing the pen patterns shown in Figure 45, and then try the alphabet illustrated in Figure 46.

The top stroke of the 'T' is often elongated to give the letter a very attractive appearance (Figure 47), and this treatment can be applied to other letters, too. If it is used at the end of words, this sort of stroke can break up the text and improve the legibility of a lettering style that may be difficult to read.

Line-fillers, patterns of dots and lightly embellished letters are also liberally scattered throughout pages of Celtic illuminated work (Figure 48). Random initial letters may be filled with colour and surrounded by small, red dots, a treatment that was often used for large letters in the Lindisfarne Gospels. The illumination in the Lindisfarne Gospels has a lighter touch than the decoration in the Book of Kells, and the letter shown in Figure 49 reveals the use of finer knotwork, lighter colouring and many surrounding and filling red-dot patterns. If you look closely at some of the original pages of text, you will find a gloss (see page 38) of Anglo-Saxon minuscule lettering between the lines of uncial text.

Figure 46: Uncial letters.

Figure 45: Pen patterns for establishing the correct angle for writing uncials.

Figure 47: An elongated 'T'.

Figure 48. Celtic line-fillers.

Figure 49: A letter 'M' from the Lindisfarne Gospels.

PROJECT: *Creating a Celtic letter 'T'*

A letter 'T' that begins the text *Tunc crucifixerant* from the Book of Kells is illustrated. A long-tailed creature, with a cat-like head and feet, forms the whole of the main part of the letter, enclosing a knotwork pattern that is fairly simple in its widest portions, but develops into a more complex, haphazard pattern around the more difficult areas of the body, although it still maintains an unbroken thread. The animal's teeth clasp a tangled mass of prey, which fills the space between its head and body.

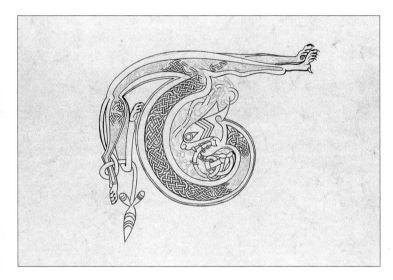

1 The letter is first traced into place and outlined.

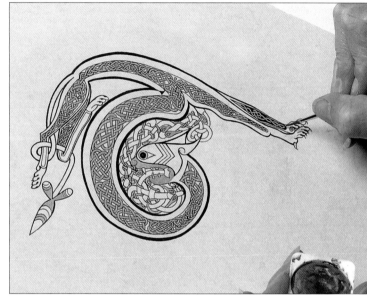

2 Next the gold and colours are added.

3 To finish, the head is overlaid with colours.

Chapter 3

In this chapter we will look at the Carolingian style of lettering and illumination that is found in such works as the Winchester Bible, a manuscript that we will use as our principal source. The description 'Carolingian' is derived from the name of Charlemagne, who was crowned king of the Franks in 771 and had great influence over arts and learning, which he promoted and patronised throughout his reign. On his death in Aachen in 814, his library was sold and the proceeds distributed amongst the needy, according to his directions. The style of lettering that we call Carolingian is considered to be the basis of the minuscule alphabet that we use today. It represents the first real attempt to create an alphabet of letters that was separate from the capitals that were used for emphasis at the beginning of verses and chapters.

CAROLINGIAN LETTERS

Although you will find that many different pieces of lettering are described as Carolingian, individual characteristics sprang from the hands of different scribes from area to area. Figure 1 shows a Carolingian alphabet that is a fairly modernised version of some of the original Carolingian styles. The ascending strokes have a thickened termination, yet there is a general simplicity to the letters. The lines of writing are widely spaced to allow plenty of room for the elongated ascenders and descenders, and at least two-and-a-half times the width of the writing lines can be left between each line of text (Figure 2). The alphabet is often written between guidelines that are only three times the width of the nib, giving the letters a squatness and strength that is very attractive. Some Carolingian texts can be quite thin and spindly in appearance, however, with a writing-line height of about six times the width of the nib (Figure 3).

If you want to recreate the appearance of the lettering that accompanies a particular manuscript exactly, you will have to take the time to study the lettering and working in order to achieve a good copy. Remember, however, that some historical texts contain lettering that has many idiosyncrasies, which can be hard to copy. In this case, rather than slavishly trying to reproduce the text word by word, it may be better simply to adapt the writing to your own style. It should then be possible to produce a good, flowing piece of lettering instead of laboriously trying to achieve what may turn out to be a very stilted reproduction.

The illuminated letters that accompanied the Carolingian script were initially fairly simple. The example shown in Figure 4 is a pen-formed letter with animal terminations at the end of each stroke. (It is thought that the elephant's head may represent Charlemagne's pet elephant Abulabaz, a gift from Caliph Haroun-al-Rachid in 802.) The manuscript, which was kept at St Denis from about 802 to 810, is today housed in the Bibliothèque Nationale in Paris, France.

The band of gold in the main stem of the 'B' consists of gold leaf on a nicely raised, gesso base. The sweeping curves of the 'B' are quite difficult to produce well and will need a lot of practice. In order to construct the letter, first make an outline drawing of it to ensure that you have formed the shape correctly. Experiment with this outline to achieve the proper pen directions for making the strokes, using the full thickness of the nib for the wider parts of the letter and tapering strokes for such thinner parts as the elephant's tusks. When you have become accustomed to forming the letter, you can either try writing it freehand, if you feel confident enough to do this, or else trace down your outline onto the vellum and use it as a guide to help you to draw the letter as accurately as possible (Figure 5)

Figure 2: The composition of the letters.

Figure 1: The Carolingian alphabet.

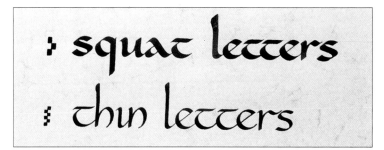

Figure 3: Squat and thin letters.

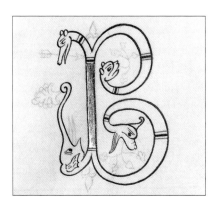

Figure 4: A letter 'B' from a ninth-century manuscript – the letter is outlined in ink, then the raised gold is applied.

Figure 5: The coloured strokes are added to complete the letter.

PROJECT: *Creating a pen-formed letter 'C'*

Using the ninth-century example that we have recreated as a guide, we can form a new set of initials in a similar style for use with any piece of lettering.

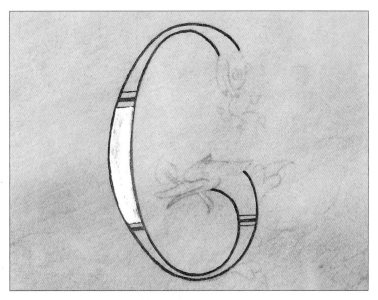

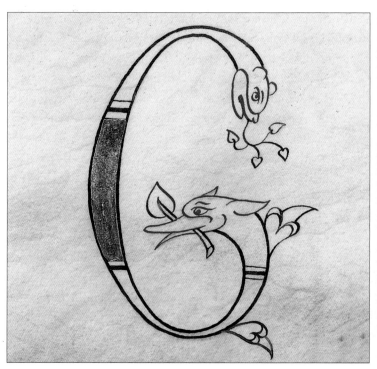

1 A letter 'C' in the same style. Make a draft letter and trace it onto the vellum. Add the inked outlines, then the gold.

2 The heads do not represent any particular animals, but instead use the general qualities of the animals in the original letter loosely to depict a variety of either real or imaginary creatures.

HLOE from the greek meaning 'a green shoot'

3 The finished letter with some Carolingian text added.

Although the letter 'N' in Figure 6 was a bit more challenging to design because it required a lot of terminal figures at the end of the uprights (Figure 7), with a little imagination any letter can be given the same treatment.

Figure 6: The outline of a letter 'N' with animal terminations is traced onto the vellum.

Figure 7: The finished letter 'N'.

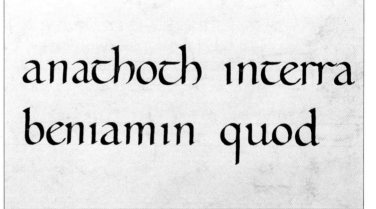

Figure 8: The lettering style used in the Winchester Bible.

The Winchester Bible

As we have already noted, many slightly different texts come under the general description 'Carolingian', including the Winchester Bible (Figure 8). During this period, all of the great churches were required to possess a copy of the Vulgate – St Jerome's translation of the Hebrew and Greek scriptures – and Henry of Blois (who was bishop of Winchester at the time), the brother of King Stephen, appears to have been the most likely person to have commissioned the work. Indeed, at the beginning of the Winchester Bible is a representation of a bishop holding a large, red volume under his arm, which further supports this theory. In addition, before Henry died, he gave money to the cathedral's scriptorium (the monks' writing room), possibly so that the work would be continued. It was not completed after his death, however: although the text, which was entirely written by one scribe, is complete, many of the illuminated letters were never finished and therefore appear in various stages of construction.

The Winchester Bible was produced in the cathedral's priory between around 1160 and 1175. It is a very large work – the vellum leaves measure 583 x 396mm (23 x 15") – and it was originally bound into two volumes, comprising 468 leaves in total. Since then, it has been rebound at least twice, once into three volumes and more recently into four, which means that four double-page spreads can be seen at once.

Some of the original letters in the Winchester Bible are missing: about nine have been identified as having been acquired by private collectors, a few of which are now on show to the public at various galleries around the world. The Bible itself, however, is believed to have spent most of its existence in Winchester and to have been loaned out for special exhibitions only seldom. It is today on display at Winchester Cathedral's Triforium Gallery, along with other illuminated manuscripts and books of importance. The pages that contain the most elaborate initials are much darker than the others, indicating that these pages have been displayed the most.

If you study the letters of the Winchester Bible carefully, you will see that the gold leaf appears to lie quite flat on the page. (Through the gold, you can often see veins on the vellum, as well as other markings on the surface, such as ruled writing lines.) Some of the unfinished letters show that the gold leaf was laid on a gesso base, and some also have the raised appearance that is normally associated with gesso. The general flatness of the gold areas is due to an extremely thin application of gesso, and the shine achieved is quite remarkable – it has survived in this beautiful condition for more than 800 years.

PROJECT: *An illuminated letter 'P'*

The illuminated letters in the Winchester Bible have an incredibly rich, vibrant quality, with beautiful, stylised ornamentation and vivid, clear colours. Figure 9 shows a reconstructed letter 'P'. It is taken from the opening page of the Second Book of Kings, and begins the sentence *Prevaricatus est Moab* ('And Moab rebelled [against Israel]'). Although this is a complex initial, we will work through the individual components of letters of this type gradually, so that the style is learnt in small portions, making larger projects less daunting.

Figure 9: A letter 'P' from the Winchester Bible.

1 The letter is drawn in outline.

2 The design is traced onto the vellum.

3 Paint gesso onto the areas to be gilded.

4 Apply the gold leaf.

5 Add the base colours, then outline the shapes.

6 Add modelling and detail with a fine brush.

Detailed study of the illumination techniques used in the Winchester Bible has enabled scholars to identify the principal illuminators, whom they have given descriptive names, such as the Master of the Leaping Figures, the Master of the Apocrypha Drawings, the Master of the Genesis Initial and so on. It is clear that two illuminators often worked on one initial, the first designing the letter and the second adding the gold and colours, as well as adapting the flow of the drapery, the facial features and other details to suit his particular style.

The 'P' in Figure 9 was worked by the Master of the Leaping Figures. It shows Elijah, who, having made prophesies and performed miracles with God's assistance, is depicted in the midst of a windstorm being taken up to heaven in a blazing chariot drawn by fiery horses. Elijah leaves behind his companion, Elisha, who asks Elijah to give him part of his spirit. As Elijah ascends to heaven, his mantle drops, and Elisha, taking up the garment, proceeds to perform miracles of his own, the men of Jericho thereby recognising that the spirit of Elijah has settled upon him. This account, which is contained in the first two chapters of the Second Book of Kings, is simply and vividly portrayed. Elisha, who is depicted watching his friend depart, holds up a scroll on which is written his parting cry, 'My father, my father, the war chariot of Israel and his horsemen'. The main bowl of the letter portrays Elijah, his feet licked by flames, being received into heaven. The stem of the letter is decorated with heavily stylised bunches of grapes that form a backdrop to the brightly coloured figures. The letter runs the full length of a page and measures approximately 45cm (17 3/4") from top to bottom (the reconstruction is of the same size).

When trying to recreate a medieval letter, it is helpful if you have some idea of the size of the original and make your work the same size, which will enable you to carry out the painting techniques properly, and as they were originally executed. Although creating a larger letter does not present much of a problem, if you try to work on a smaller scale you may find some of the detailing very difficult to achieve. When you have fully understood a particular style's method of construction, you can design differently sized pieces in full knowledge of the limitations that you may thereby be imposing on your painting and gilding.

FIGURES, DRAPERY, TREES, PLANTS AND STYLISED PATTERNS IN THE WINCHESTER BIBLE

The human figures depicted in the Winchester Bible's illuminated letters have been given a very stylised treatment, with exaggerated folds to their drapery and thin, elegant limbs. (Fig.ure 10 shows a figure of a man contained in the initial letter 'H' at the beginning of the Book of Exodus.) Bright orange, green, deep pink and blue are the principal colours that have been used for the clothing, and the robes often have thin, gold edges. Hair is made up of a neat series of curls that have been carefully painted and outlined. Parts of the body have received the same linear treatment as the clothing, while green tints have often been added to the flesh colours.

Figure 10: A stylised human figure.

Figure 11: A stylised tree.

Trees and plants have been heavily stylised, too. The tree (Figure 11), which has been taken from a letter 'U' in the Book of Jeremiah, demonstrates the stylised treatment of vines, with their large bunches of grapes. Note that the branches have been portrayed as growing from pockets in the trunk of the plant. Figures are sometimes depicted standing on rocks, or perched on part of the letter, but they can also appear as if they were floating within the design, having been given no footing at all.

Attractive bands of patterning have been used everywhere to form parts of the upright or curved portions of the letters, for example, the scalloped band running down the upright of a letter 'F' (Figure 12). (The repeating pattern of the scallop, flanked by curving arches that terminate in a tight coil, can be continued in a full border if necessary.) The background is black, as is usual for most multicoloured strips of pattern, while the scallops are alternately coloured a deep, reddish pink (obtained from a mixture of madder carmine and white), bright cadmium orange, scarlet, cobalt blue and green. Each piece on the black background has been coloured before being shaded with a darker shade of the same colour. Thin white highlights have then been added.

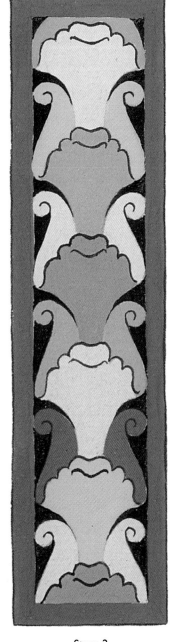
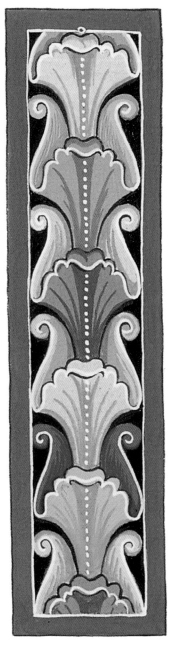

Stage 1   Stage 2   Stage 3

Figure 12: A pattern formed using scallop shapes.

Figures13–14 are part of a letter that is composed of a double band of gold bars interwoven with scrollwork. The scrollwork doubles back and forth, revealing different-coloured sides with each fold, the topsides in blue and green and the undersides in orange and purple. Red scallop shapes have been painted between each set of folds on the black background. Figure 15 illustrates another portion of the same letter, which has wide, curved pieces of pattern folding around the outside of the gold bars before joining to form a floral centrepiece. This pattern is repeated to fill the required area. Figure 16 also uses

double bands of gold, with a simple inner pattern of orange scallop shapes, followed by diagonally divided portions in alternating colours of green, blue and red separating each scallop. Figures 17–18 show the construction of a geometric pattern, whose diamond-shaped boxes of alternating colours give a three-dimensional appearance to the strip of pattern. The black background has been overpainted with gold flowers.

Some of the patterns in the Winchester Bible are based on shades of one colour, such as the portion of a letter 'O' shown in Figure 19.

Figure 13: Double gold bars and coloured scrolls are used to form this pattern.

Figure 14: Outlines and modelling are added.

Figure 15: Constructing a pattern of double bars with floral centres.

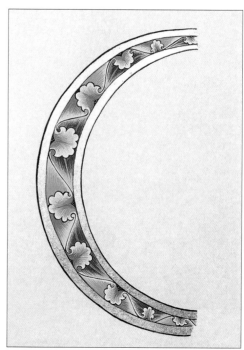

Figure 16: Double bars with scallops.

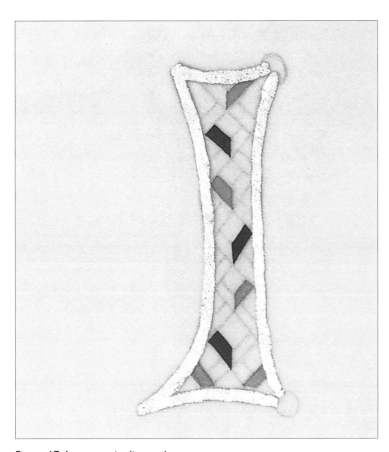

Figure 17: A geometric diamond pattern.

Figure 18: The colours are outlined and the final detail is added.

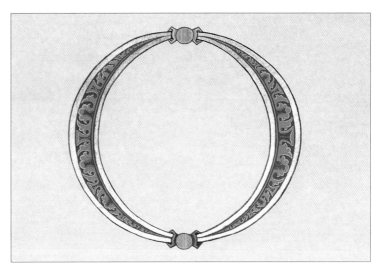

Figure 19: A pattern in shades of one colour.

The design has been painted on a pinkish-red background, then over-painted with paler-pink scallops between shapes that terminate in alternate red and blue tips. White highlights have been added to complete the pattern.

More detail has often been added outside the main portion of the letter by means of interesting terminal points to various parts of the letter. The terminals to an 'E' (shown in Figure 20) are in stylised floral work, while those in Figure 21 have animal and human heads. Lattices of interweaving bands may also be used to terminate letters and connect strokes (Figure 22).

Figure 20: Stylised floral terminations are given to this letter 'E'.

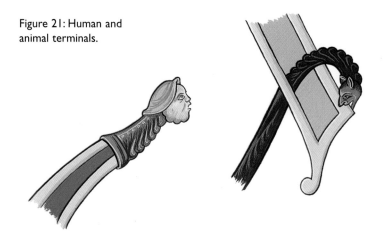

Figure 21: Human and animal terminals.

Figure 22: Lattice terminals.

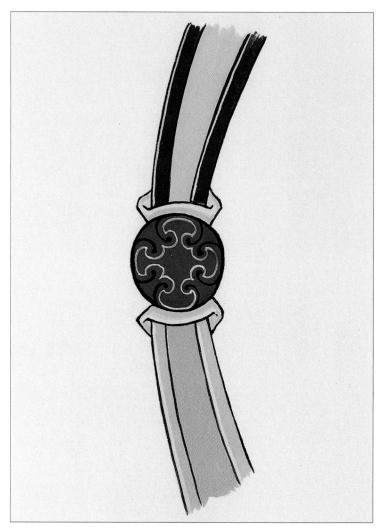

Figure 23: Knots.

Another neat design feature is the small knot or decorative flower that is used to tie two bands of pattern or parts of a design together (Figure 23). These devices are usually placed on the curved parts of letters, as you can see at the top and bottom of the 'O' in Figure 19, as well as the orange knots on the 'P' in Figure 9. The heads of animals and people are also used in this way, as can be seen in the centre of the 'B' in figures 25–26.

Figure 24: Interlocking versals.

The initial letters themselves are large versal letters that are extremely regularly shaped and well balanced. (The complete versal alphabet will be covered in more detail in Chapter 5.) Smaller red, blue and green capital letters accompany many of the illuminated initials, making up the remainder of the phrase or title piece. In contrast to the superb quality of the illuminated letters, however, in the Winchester Bible many of these capital letters have been rather poorly executed. Their placing within words to fit the available space nevertheless makes interesting patterns and contributes to the whole design (Figure 24).

Figure 25: This illuminated letter 'B' is based on a fine example in the Winchester Bible. Transfer leaf is applied, then the base colours are added.

Figure 26: Coloured versal letters are used for the words needing emphasis.

DESIGNING YOUR OWN PIECES

By working on the various components of letters, such as those that appear in the Winchester Bible, you will gradually build up an understanding of the techniques that were used, as well as the style of the illuminated letters. You will then be able to design new letters for your own pieces of lettering.

The illuminated piece shown in Figure 28 starts with an initial letter that is based on a 'B' that opens the Book of Psalms. The central scenes illustrate the text, which consists of coloured versal capitals and Carolingian lettering. The whole letter is surrounded by a narrow border of pale green, a treatment that is given to many of the letters in the Winchester Bible.

Designs in this style tend to be the most successful when they are contained within a fairly compact area. The versals were carefully fitted into the piece's required width by using overlapping and reduced-size letters. Not only did this give a pleasing effect, but it also ensured that exactly the right amount of space was used. The size of the black text was also chosen to fit the space available, in order to give a neat, compact design.

Figure 27: Fine detail is added to the rock.

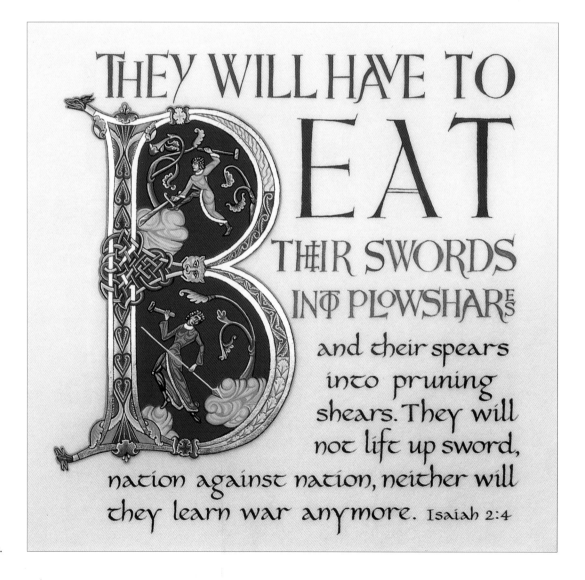

Figure 28: The completed piece.

Chapter 4

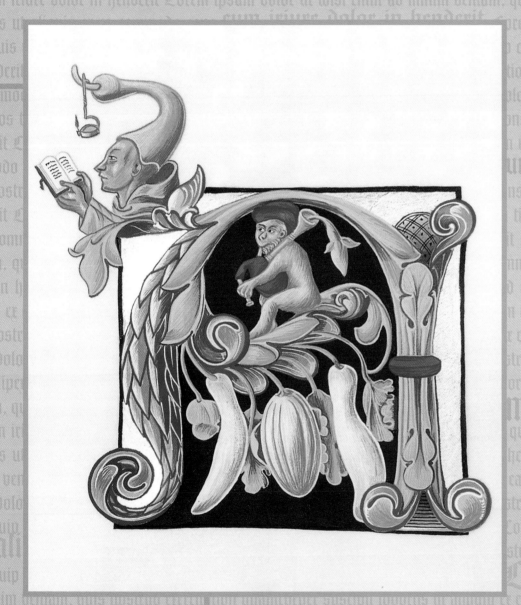

A variety of terms are used to describe the components of illuminated letters, and we will cover a selection of them in this chapter, mainly concentrating on those that date from the Gothic period. The Gothic period, which lasted from the late twelfth to the early sixteenth centuries, has given us a rich selection of styles and types of ornamentation for illuminated letters.

GOTHIC DECORATION

TYPES OF INITIAL LETTERS

The decorated initial

The decorated initial, which contains no human or animal figures, is the most straightforward type of illuminated letter. The letter is embellished by extending and elaborating some of its strokes, so that they intertwine with both themselves and each other to form a decorative unit. Figure 5 on page 16 illustrates this type of illumination for a simple letter 'H', while Figure 1 shows a decorated letter 'P' with a floral interior. Although these examples are quite simple, the decoration may also be incredibly complex, as can be seen in some of the great insular manuscripts, like the well-known letter 'X' in folio 34R of the Book of Kells, as well as another 'X' in folio 29R of the Lindisfarne Gospels.

The inhabited initial

The term 'inhabited initial' is used to describe an initial that contains figures or animals that do not depict a specific scene. The figures are usually intertwined with scrollwork emanating from the extremities of the letter, and some charming and lively patterns are often the result (Figure 2).

The historiated initial

Historiated initials first appeared in illuminated manuscripts written in the insular style in about 750 and became very popular during the medieval period. They contain a recognisable scene, usually relating to the text. The 'D' in Figure 3, for example, depicts Christ making a blessing. (This letter is taken from a page of the Grey-FitzPayn

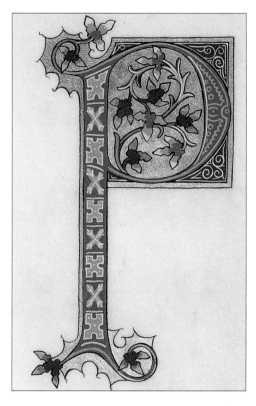

Figure 1: A decorated initial 'P'.

Hours that was created between about 1300 and 1308 and can now be seen at the Fitzwilliam Museum in Cambridge, England.) Many well-known stories from the Bible may be portrayed, a particular favourite being that of David and Goliath, as illustrated in Figure 4. This example has been recreated from the French original contained in the *La Charité* Psalter (folio 51b), which dates from the end of the twelfth century. Whole borders can be historiated with a series of scenes that recount a particular event or a series of related events.

Figure 2: An inhabited initial 'R'.

Figure 3: A historiated initial 'D'.

Figure 4: A historiated initial 'B'.

TYPES OF ORNAMENTATION

Diapering

Diapering is a type of ornamentation that involves the painting of a tiny – often repeating – pattern over a letter's background surface. The term is derived from the French word *diapre*, which means 'variegated'. It is very attractive type of ornamentation that is characteristic of medieval illumination (having been used as early as the eleventh century) and that is a common feature of Gothic art, too.

The pattern used in the above-mentioned letter 'D' (Figure 3) is a blue, red and white design that is built up as shown in Figure 5. The background is painted dark blue and is then divided with a grid of black squares. Small, white squares are painted in the centre of every other square, which are joined diagonally from corner to corner. Red squares are painted into the other boxes, which have been finished off with a central white dot. The pattern is simple, but effective, giving a rich depth to the design. The background of the letter is gold leaf, which should be applied before any paint is added so that the gold does not stick to the gum that the paint contains.

Diaper patterns can be divided into three groups: geometric, floral and embossed (or gold) patterns.

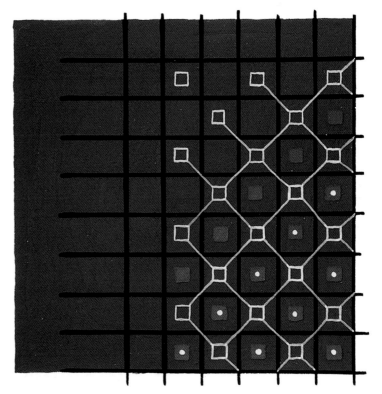

Figure 5: A simple geometric diaper.

PROJECT: *Creating a fifteenth-century geometric diaper design*

Figure 8 shows a geometric diaper design taken from a page of the Hours of Peter II, Duke of Brittany, which was created between 1455 and 1457. Every other box has been painted gold, and three other colours - red, blue and sepia - have also been used. The resultant pattern is a series of alternating diagonal lines which rises to the middle of the area that will covered and then descends to the outsides.

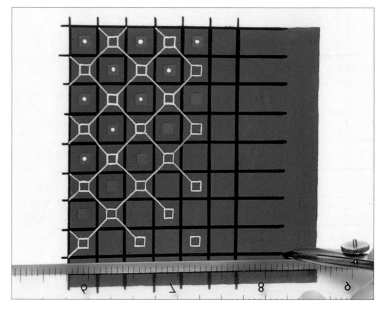

Figure 8: A ruling pen can be used for the partition lines of diaper patterns. Here it is shown ruling the lines for the diaper pattern shown in Figure 5.

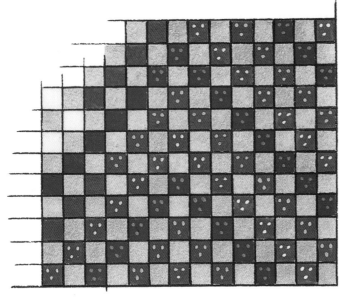

Figure 6: Red, blue and sepia diaper.

1 Draw a framework of vertical and horizontal lines, with the lines at a distance of about 5mm (3/16") apart (see Figure 6). Find the central square of one of the top rows and start painting in the relevant row of squares to either side with one of the colours, in this case red. Remember to leave the next two rows beneath this one blank for the other colours. Calculate which rows in the rest of the grid of squares will need to be the same colour and then paint them. Using the next colour, blue, paint the row of squares below the red. Now use the final colour, sepia, to paint the remaining blank squares, so that you have filled the whole grid.

2 Add a pattern of three dots to each of the coloured squares using a lighter shade of the background colour. Having been lightened with white, the sepia has also been mixed with a touch of lemon yellow to brighten the colour a little.

Figure 7: Fill the ruling pen with a brush.

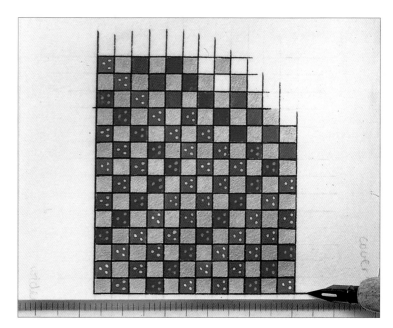

Figure 9: Mapping pen and rule.

3 Use a ruling pen (Figure 7) and black paint to draw in the dividing lines. Ruling pens are available from art shops and are simple to use in conjunction with a rule. Set the ends to the required width and then fill the gap between them with paint. Draw the pen along the rule's bevelled edge, but make sure that the paint does not come into contact with the ruler itself (Figure 8). Take care not to make the black paint too thin, as the painted surfaces over which you will be ruling will be very porous. If too much paint, or paint that is too thin, is drawn over other painted areas, it could flood out of the pen too quickly and cause the lines to be thick or blotchy. Alternatively, you could use a mapping pen and rule (Figure 9).

CREATING A
DIAMOND-SHAPED AND PERSPECTIVE DIAPER

The diaper pattern shown in Figure 10 is taken from a page of the St Omer Hours, which was created in around 1350 in northern France. The overall effect is of circles and squares, the joined white lines giving the red-crossed boxes the appearance of rounded corners.

This pattern is most easily achieved by painting the whole area to be diapered with the background colour, in this instance a pale pink. Draw a grid of squares over the background and then use red paint to rule in all of the boxes with fairly thick lines. Give every other square a red cross. Add a small, white, linear box to the centre of each of the remaining boxes. Join the corners of each white box throughout the design.

The diamond-shaped diaper illustrated in Figure 11 comes from the Hours of Mary of Guelders, dated 1415. This design, with its alternate, vertical rows of red and blue between gold rows, is a good example of how diamonds must be accurately drawn so that they appear in neat lines one above the other. When drawing the grid for the diaper, be sure to make the angle of all of the diagonal lines the same, because if you do not draw the two sets of lines at the same number of degrees from vertical the diamond shapes will not be correct and will slant sideways to form unpleasant shapes. Also try to ensure that the rows of diamonds are parallel with the sides of the page that you are working on.

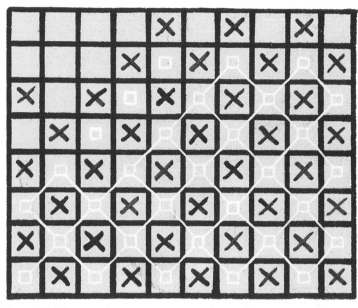

Figure 10: A fourteenth-century geometric diaper.

It is often better to work on diaper patterns before painting other areas of the work so that you can neaten up any untidy edges. The figures that appear immediately below the diapered area have headdresses that should have smooth edges, for example, and these can be painted in accurately when the diaper is complete.

Perspective is achieved in medieval miniatures by the use of diapered floors. The Hours of Giangaleazzo Visconti, Duke of Milan, which dates from about 1388 to 1395, contains some very elaborate historiated initials, as well as displaying much use of diapered backgrounds. A fine initial 'D' from folio 115 depicts King David sitting beneath a canopy. The floor was created using the diaper pattern shown in Figure 12, and its sepia-coloured background has alternate, linear squares of red and white, with counterchanged dots in each square. When recreating this pattern, first draw the grid on a

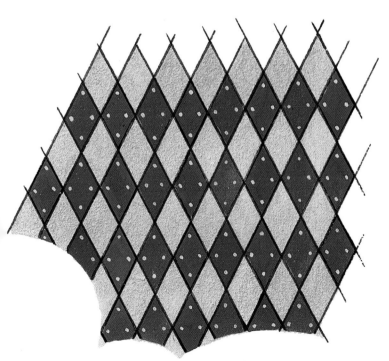

Figure 11: Diamond-shaped diaper.

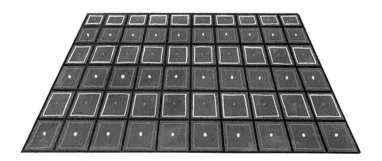

Figure 12: Perspective diaper.

separate sheet of paper so that the horizon point can be marked and the lines drawn to meet it. Draw the horizontal lines parallel to the top edge of the paper and then trace the necessary lines onto the area to be diapered (Figure 13).

The same illuminated letter also contains two other diaper patterns: one (detailed below) is completely floral, while the other is a pattern of flowers arranged in a geometric layout on a red screen behind King David. Small red and blue flowers tipped with white (Figure 14) have been painted over the red background in regular rows. This manuscript also contains some attractive line-fillers, which will be discussed later in the chapter.

The pale-coloured diaper shown in Figure 15 consists of a grid of

Figure 13: Horizon lines are used to form the perspective correctly.

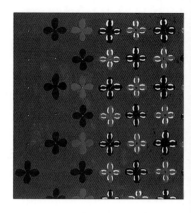

Figure 14: Geometric diaper with regularly spaced flowers.

PROJECT: *Planning a decorated and diapered initial letter*

The initial 'N' illustrated in Figure 16 is a decorated initial that has a diapered background of blue and gold checks (shown in greater detail in step 1). Letters of this type, which have a simple, central feature – in this case, a shield – on a diapered background, are common. The letter is typically set within a box that is usually bordered with gold, or another colour, and the extremities of the letter have been given floral terminations. These floral terminations can be extended to form whole borders in the same style (borders in general will be looked at further in Chapter 7).

1 The construction of the central diaper pattern.

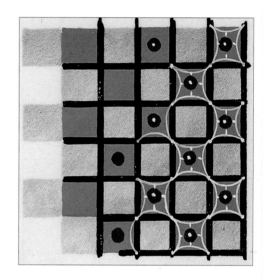

Figure 16: A letter 'N' with diapered centre and shield.

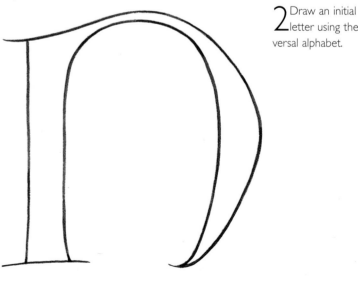

2 Draw an initial letter using the versal alphabet.

thin red lines separating pale-blue and green squares. Each square has been lined with another red square, after which dark-green triangles have been placed within each pale-green square and small, red circles within each pale-blue square. This pattern is found in the *Belle Heures* of John, Duke of Berry, folio 30.

Floral diaper designs

The corners of the 'D' mentioned previously have a delicate gold floral diaper on a dark-blue background (Figure 18). The scrolling foliage has been carefully adapted to fit the required spaces. Each corner of the letter contains a shield, around which the diaper has been fitted and neatly worked into the confined spaces.

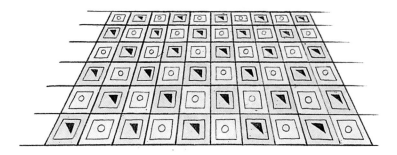

Figure 15: Pale-green and blue squares with thin red lines form this perspective diaper.

3 Now add the corner terminations.

4 Square off the letter with a surrounding box.

5 Add an outer second line and work the left-hand ends of the box into the floral sections using curved fillers, as shown. Give the whole of the left-hand edge of the box this treatment.

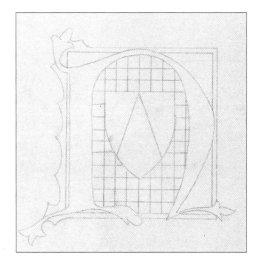

6 Draw the central features and work out any diaper patterns. The letter is now ready to paint.

Figure 17: Guidelines are traced onto the dark background.

Figure 18: Gold on blue floral diaper.

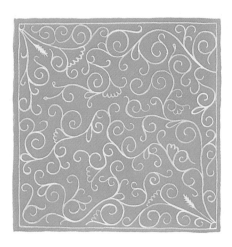

Figure 19: White diaper over a dark ground.

When recreating this diaper, paint the blue background first (Figure 17). Having designed the diaper pattern on tracing paper, transfer it to the background. (When the background colours are dark, the tracing can be difficult to see, but if you work at an angle, so that the light shines on the traced lines, they will show up well enough to be followed accurately.) Finally, working along the traced outline, paint over the background colour in gold (Figure 18).

The background of the large initial 'B' (which is taken from the *La Charité* Psalter that was mentioned previously) has a fine, white, floral diaper over a dark background (Figure 19). As described above, create the design on tracing paper before transferring it to the work. You will achieve a much more even, well-arranged spread of curls if you work them out in advance rather than trying to paint them directly onto the work freehand.

Figure 20, which is taken from a fourteenth-century French manuscript, has a light, coiling diaper on a red background. The coils are composed of two parallel lines, with small shoots of three short strokes branching off at regular intervals. The remaining gaps have been filled with small dots. The same colour scheme was employed for the diaper shown in Figure 21. This is a looser, more open, pattern, consisting of main branches to which are attached twisting leaves. (A similar pattern, in which gold appears on a dark-green background, was used in the same fifteenth-century French manuscript.) Gold on blue was used for the pattern taken from a fifteenth-century missal that is illustrated in Figure 22, which incorporates flower heads amongst the branches and leaves.

Figure 20: Gold floral diaper on a red ground.

Figure 21: A more open floral diaper.

Figure 22: Gold floral diaper on a blue ground.

Embossed diaper designs

Diaper patterns can be embossed on paint or gold, a technique that is most successful on raised gilding, where the gesso can be impressed with the design. The easiest embossed patterns to make are those that are based on a geometric design, so that the lines can be accurately scored into the gold (Figure 23). Scored lines that make up a grid often have small, floral motifs in each section (Figure 24). The sharp edges reflect the light well and also highlight the contrast of light and shade.

Curving patterns are more difficult to score into the gold smoothly, and can sometimes look a little ragged. The floral pattern – taken from a late thirteenth-century French manuscript – shown in Figure 25 should be very carefully impressed, with care being taken that the gold is not scratched off or the gesso cracked as a result of too much pressure having been applied. A pencil burnisher can be used to make simple dot patterns (Figure 26).

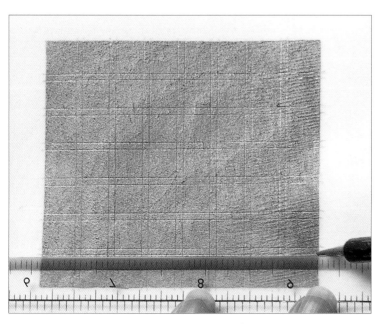

Figure 23: Embossed geometric diaper on gold paint.

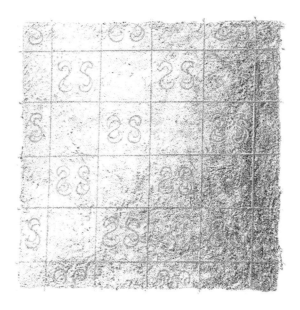

Figure 24: Embossed geometric diaper with scroll detail on gold leaf.

Figure 25: Floral embossed diaper.

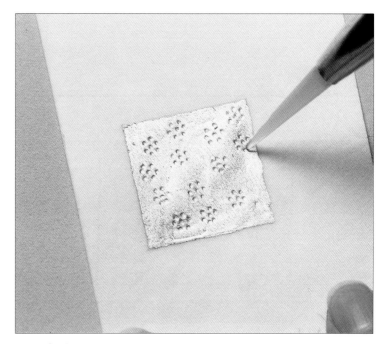

Figure 26: Dot-pattern diaper.

DROLLERIES AND GROTESQUES

Drolleries are amusing figures that appear in manuscripts dating from as early as the insular period. They were particularly popular from the thirteenth to the fifteenth centuries. Illustrated here is an example taken from a fifteenth-century Italian gradual (now to be seen at the J Paul Getty Museum, Malibu, California, USA) that depicts a monkey playing the bagpipes. The colours of this piece are particularly striking (figures 27–28).

Grotesques are hybrid forms of creature, usually of a comic nature, composed of a mixture of human and animal forms. They are frequently seen in Gothic illumination and often bear no obvious relationship to the accompanying text: they appear in all sorts of places, apparently just for fun, and have no clear meaning. Small grotesques can also be found tucked into corners and attached to the ends of letters.

The fourteenth-century Luttrell Psalter (which is today housed in the British Library) contains many such examples (Figure 29). The lettering in the Luttrell Psalter is a handsome, Gothic script that displays the angular strokes common to all of the Gothic styles, as well as squared feet to the letters. Figures 30-31 shows the alphabet used, along with another, variant alphabet, in a similar style, that accompanied texts throughout the Gothic period. Smaller illuminated letters are spread throughout the text, some examples of which are illustrated in figure 30.

Figure 27: An initial 'N' with a 'drollery' monkey is traced onto the vellum. The flat gold leaf is added, then the colours can be painted in.

Figure 28: Vivid colours give this letter a lot of character.

Figure 29: Grotesques found in the Luttrell Psalter.

Figure 30: Lettering found in the Luttrell Psalter – a.

Figure 31: Lettering in the Luttrell Psalter – b.

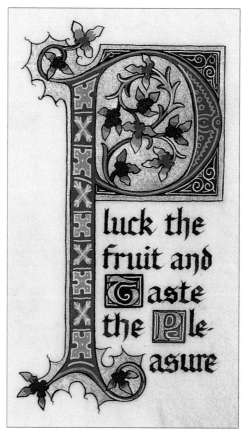

Figure 32: Small illuminated initials used in text blocks.

BESTIARIES

Bestiaries, or books of beasts, date from medieval times and were very popular during the twelfth and thirteenth centuries, especially in England. Because few illuminators were well enough travelled to have had much knowledge of the animal kingdom throughout the world, a strange array of beasts is depicted in such books, their descriptions having been gleaned from a mixture of classical renditions and recounted tales – both real and imaginary – of beasts seen by travellers, as well as animals of which the artist had first-hand knowledge. Many of the animals that featured in such works were based on a Greek text called *Physiologus* ('The Natural Philosopher'), which was possibly created in Alexandria during the second century AD. Nearly 50 creatures and plants were described within its pages, and it was translated into many languages and referred to frequently.

Animals were often depicted in borders that accompanied illuminated initials and text, and some are shown in figures 33-34. A scene containing animals often appeared along the bottom of an illuminated page from the thirteenth century onwards (such 'bottom-of-the-page' scenes are termed *bas-de-page*, whether or not they contain animals or any other type of illustration).

Figure 33: Beasts of the chase.

Figure 34: A hunting scene.

GRISAILLE AND CAMAIEU

Grisaille is a painting technique that employs only shades of grey for an illustration (the term grisaille is derived from the French word for grey, *gris*). It was more often used for illuminated scenes than for letters (Figure 35).

Camaieu is a similar method of illumination, in that it employs a single colour in varying shades, and letters worked in this manner can be very attractive (Figure 36). Camaieu equates to the same technique as that used in Celtic work, in which one background colour is overlaid with darker shades of the same colour.

Figure 35: Grisaille.

Figure 36: Camaieu.

LINE-FILLERS

Line-fillers, which were often used in Gothic illumination, usually take the form of solid, bold-coloured strips of filler placed at the end of any line of text that does not fill the available page width. A selection of line-fillers, taken from various Gothic manuscripts, is shown in Figure 37.

Diaper patterns were also used to form line-fillers, and animals were incorporated into them, too. A set of gold-burnished line-fillers (Figure 38) appears in the Hours of Giangaleazzo Visconti mentioned above.

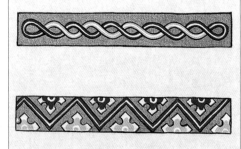

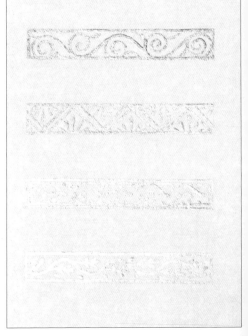

Figure 37: Gothic line-fillers.

Figure 38: Gold line-fillers.

Chapter 5

From the late twelfth century, a very intricate, filigree type of penwork, called *littera florissa*, or 'pen-flourished' lettering, was used to decorate some of the smaller capital letters on large pages of text. Although letters of this type were usually only used as secondary illuminations accompanying much larger, and more elaborate, initials, they were sometimes given a greater degree of prominence. By the sixteenth century, filigree-penworked types of illumination had practically disappeared, in favour of the much bolder, heavier styles of the Renaissance. Yet this pleasing style remains worth studying.

PEN-FLOURISHED LETTERS

The pages of manuscript books have very large margins, and this form of decoration was usually carried well into the borders – and often right to the edges – of the page. Figure 1 shows an extremely elongated letter 'A', the decoration of which is carried to the bottom of the page. Other letters have decoration that runs between paragraphs of text or into the side borders, such as the 'O' and 'V' illustrated in Figure 2. These examples are taken from a manuscript that was created in Paris between about 1180 and 1190 and that is today housed at Durham Cathedral. The pages illustrated form part of the Old Testament Book of Isaiah.

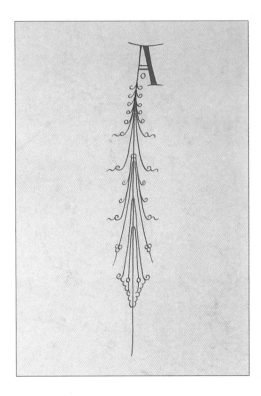

Figure 1: An elongated pen-flourished 'A'.

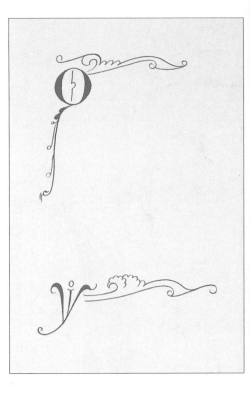

Figure 2: Horizontally pen-flourished letters 'O' and 'V'.

PROJECT: *Creating a pen-flourished pattern for use with initial letters*

You will need a small-sized calligraphy nib, such as a William Mitchell size 5, to create this sort of decoration. It is very important that you work on a really smooth surface when drawing these decorative strokes, as an uneven surface will result either in ragged lines, snaggings of the pen or ink blots. If you are using vellum, make sure that it has been well pounced, so that any waxiness or grease has been removed from the surface. A paper called 'Elephanthide' – a good imitation of vellum – is perfect for this type of work, because it has a very smooth surface

1 The pattern around the letter is built up of a combination of basic strokes. Spirals that curve inwards and terminate in a circle are used as the basis of most central portions of letters.

2 Loops are added to the spirals and are then usually filled with a small, unconnected, central loop or circle.

3 Clusters of loops are linked to the body of the decoration

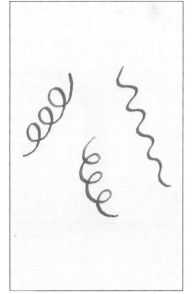

4 Long, straight strokes are drawn from the curved pieces to run down the margin. Always break off and then recommence a stroke if your pen is working at the wrong angle. Trying to push a nib backwards can have disastrous results, especially if you are applying a lot of pressure. Although you can get away with pushing a small nib backwards (the ink will still flow reasonably well), not only is this a bad habit to fall into, but it will not work when you are using a larger nib size. Take care that you blend the recommenced stroke with the halted section carefully, so that the whole appears to be a smooth, uninterrupted stroke.

5 The long, straight strokes terminate in either a small, corkscrew-like set of curls or a waving, zigzag line. The pen will only make these small flourishes well when it is moving in a particular direction, which means that this will sometimes dictate the type of finish that you will give the stroke. Alternatively, you can turn the page to enable you to use the pen at the correct angle for the particular pattern that you want to use in a certain place.

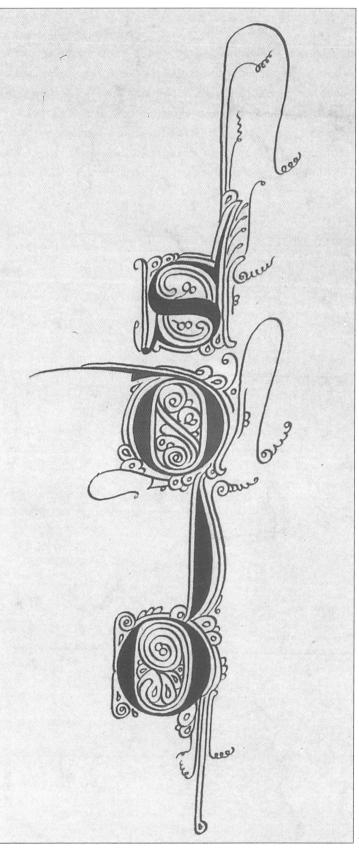

6 Small, frilled patterns can be added so that they run either along the edge of another stroke or parallel to it, without touching it. Small filler loops and extra lines can be added as required until the pattern has gradually been built up to cover the whole area.

7 Letters can easily be linked down the length of the page to give the appearance of a continuous border. Counterchanged letters and decoration, such as the red and blue letters illustrated here, give a nice effect.

PROJECT: *Decorated pen-flourished initials*

The letters used for this type of decoration are quite simple, and
their corners and centres give the starting points for the penwork.
A bold, jagged line often divides the letter into two colours, each of
a solid hue, such as blue and red (Figure 3). The 'D' illustrated here
is taken from the Hours of Philip the Good, Duke of Burgundy,
which can be seen at The Hague's Koninklijke Bibliotheek in The
Netherlands. This manuscript measures 27 x 19cm (10 10/16 x 7"),
and without its decoration the letter is about 4cm (1 9/16") square.

Figure 3: Versal letters were often divided with a jagged line into red and
blue divisions.

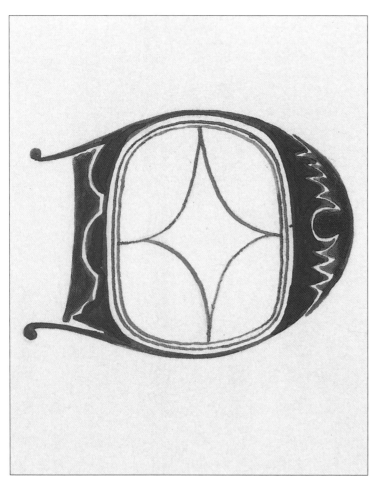

| The centre of the 'D' is divided into four portions.

2 These are gradually filled with patterns of lines and circles.

3 Straight lines are added to the outer area to form the square that will be patterned.

4 The square is then filled with similar lines and circles.

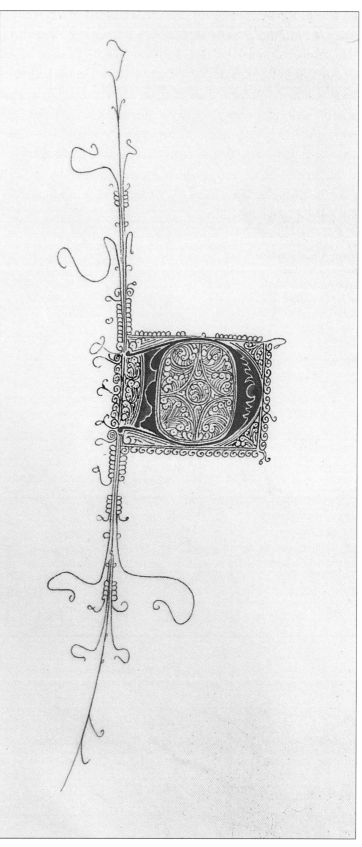

5 Finally, the outer decoration is added to finish the letter.

The 'L' shown in Figure 4 is another example of a letter that has been given a red and blue, zigzagged division. It is based on a letter contained in a manuscript at the Bibliothèque Nationale in Paris, dated 1213. A divided initial 'D', this time from a Dutch book of hours, also appears in Figure 5. Dated 1520, it was made much later than the preceding examples, and although the main letter is very similar to its predecessors, a difference can be seen in the surrounding penwork: as well as being a little more symmetrically arranged, the filled portions in parts of the flourished work accentuate the design.

In large pages of text, paragraphs were indicated by the sign shown in Figure 6. These signs appear many times in manuscripts containing pen-flourished letters.

Figure 4: Red and blue divisions are used again for this letter 'L' with penworked decoration.

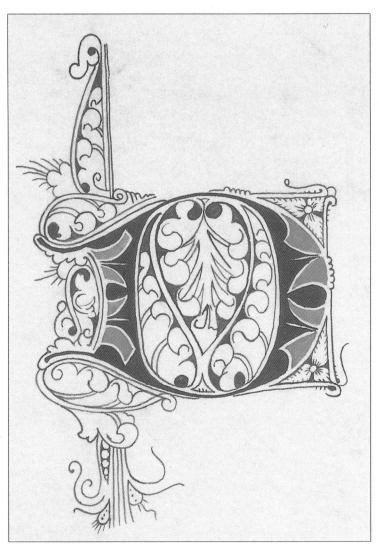

Figure 5: A Dutch letter 'D' in a similar style, but from a later period.

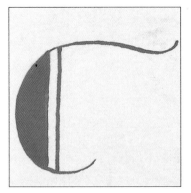

Figure 6: A paragraph sign.

Figure 7: A thirteenth-century pen-flourished 'M'.

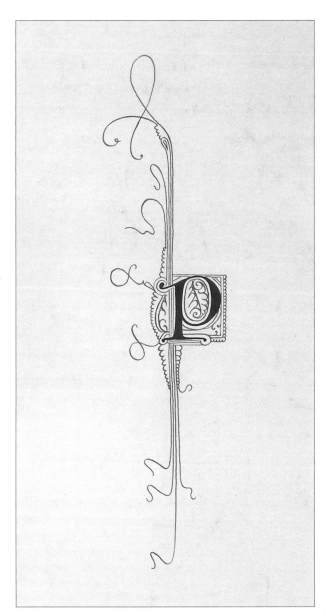

Figure 8: This pen-flourished 'P' dates from *circa* 1470.

Figure 9: Stylised floral penwork is used to decorate the lower letter 'Q' accompanying the more familiar penworked 'Q' above.

Figure 7. shows a letter 'M' that is filled with pen-flourished work and is based on an example taken from the Canticles of Alfonso the Wise (the king of Spain from 1252 to 1284), that can today be admired at the Real Biblioteca, El Escorial, Spain. The letter formed part of a music manuscript or song book, Alfonso having been a collector and writer of songs, as well as a patron of the arts. The decoration is very finely drawn, and presents a pleasing contrast to the accompanying, heavily painted, miniature portrait of a musician.

An attractive letter 'P' can be seen in a manuscript of theological texts and sermons that was written in about 1470 in Schwäbisch Gmünd, and that is now the Pierpont Morgan Library, New York

(Figure 8).

Pen decoration sometimes developed into stylised floral work (Figure 9), in which the pen was used to draw stems from some of the letters, flowers and seed heads then being attached. These motifs alternated with the usual penwork flourishes that can be seen on other letters in the same margin.

Pen-flourished versal letters

The versal letters in blocks of text illustrated with *littera florissa* usually all have the same intricate surround of penwork, and some protrude well into the block of text, a useful device for breaking up large areas of black text.

PROJECT: *Constructing versal letters*

Versal letters are constructed as shown in Figure 10. This alphabet shows the letters, which have been written with a pen, in their plainest form. For the height shown – about 25mm (1") – they should be constructed with a fairly small-sized nib, such as that used for the pen flourishes (a William Mitchell size 4 or 5).

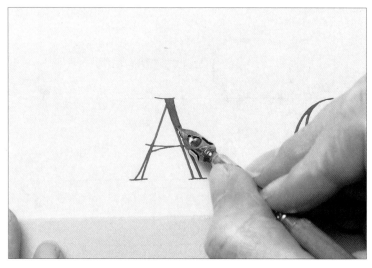

1 First draw the outside edges of the letters and then fill the centres with ink or colour, either using the nib or, if the letters are very large, a brush.

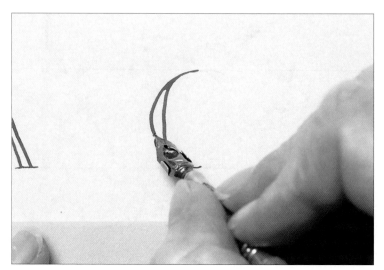

2 When drawing the curved parts of the letters, form the inner curve first. Doing this makes it easier to give a good overall shape to the letters than if the outer stroke is made first. Most of these letters are formed with the pen held at a very shallow angle, almost horizontal to the bottom edge of the page. As far as you can, try to maintain the horizontal position of the pen for the curved strokes. A little latitude is needed here and there in order to make pleasing shapes, but remember that the character of the letters will be lost if the angle is allowed to become too steep.

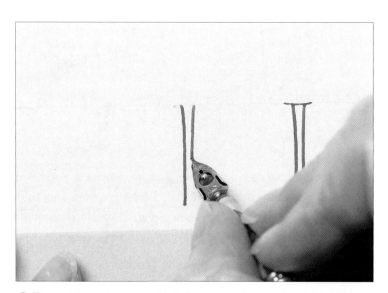

3 The upright strokes taper slightly from top to bottom, narrowing towards the centre and then widening at the foot of the stroke. The very thin, horizontal strokes at the top and base of some of the letters are made with the pen held at the same angle, but moving from side to side. The lines curve very slightly as the pen glides across from left to right in a slight, natural arc.

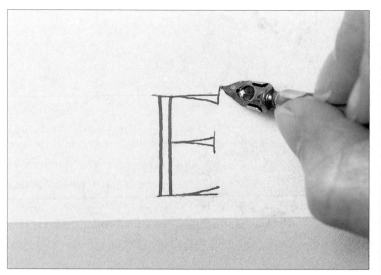

4 The strokes that close the ends of such letters as 'E' and 'F' are made with the pen turned completely round, so that the nib is vertical to the page. It can sometimes be easier to form these strokes by turning the page at an angle to achieve a very thin line, but if you do this make sure that you keep the strokes upright. Until you are confident of producing them well freehand, it is worth drawing pencil guidelines for these letters.

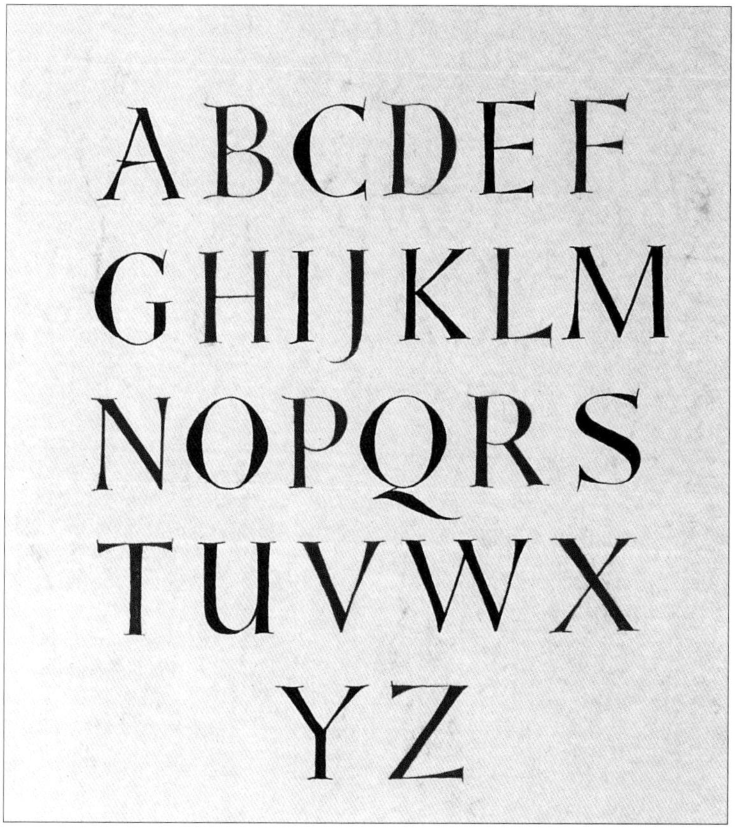

Figure 16 is based on a letter 'A' taken from Lydgate's *Life of St Edmund*, an English manuscript that dates from around 1433. The initial is coloured gold, with counterchanged red and blue areas overpainted with fine white lines. In this case, the penwork emanates from the corners of the box that surrounds the letter, and is made with a very fine nib. The penwork decoration is further embellished by the use of raised gold dots and green paint.

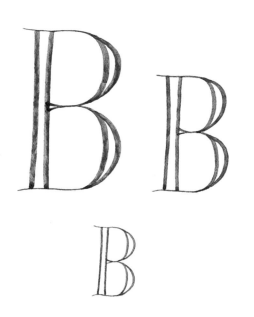

Figure 11: A letter 'B' written in three different nib sizes.

Figure 12: A letter 'R' written with the same-sized nib, but in three different sets of proportions.

Figure 13: Large blocks of versals were often interlocked and combined in a variety of sizes to fill the available space and create a pleasing effect.

ABCDEF GHIJKLM NOPQRS TUVWX YZ

Figure 10: Versal alphabet.

Most large versals that are used as decorated initials are drawn and painted, being both too large to be pen-made and often composed of complex strips of pattern, but, when writing the letters with a pen, use a size of nib that is appropriate to the letter's size. Figure 11 shows three different-sized letter 'B's, which have been left unfilled to show the construction of their outlines. They were made with a size 2, 3 and 4 William Mitchell nib respectively.

The shape of any letter can be distorted to fit the available space. Letters that have been squashed into rather short, wide shapes to fit below larger scenes and painted miniatures are particularly common in old manuscripts. The 'R' in Figure 12 is shown with additional versions that have been widened and elongated. As described in Chapter 3, versals were sometimes used in large blocks and were worked into each other in interesting ways, as is illustrated in Figure 13.

Historically, basic versal letters have been elaborated on in many different ways to produce illuminated initials. The letters have usually been made more rounded when they are enlarged, and some of the variants are shown in Figure 14. The curving of such letters as 'E', 'M' and 'T' lends itself to the addition of floral work, which can be made to sprout from any of the terminal points of the letters (Figure 15). It also gives centres to letters, which can then be filled to produce an attractive effect.

Many other styles of letter that have been written and decorated with a pen rather than a brush can also be seen. The reconstruction of the letter 'H', dating from about 1330, in Figure 17 is an attractive mixture of curved and straight strokes. Some parts of the design have been filled to give the decoration a little more strength. Figure 18, a copy of a letter 'D' that was made with a very fine pen, and its accompanying, elongated border, dates from about 1480.

An interesting set of letters is found in a scribe's specimen sheet that was made in 1447 in Münster (it can today be seen in the Koninklijke Bibliotheek, The Hague). In these examples, the pen flourishes have been worked around letters composed of broad pen strokes. The main strokes of the letters are set apart and mostly unconnected, being instead linked by the filigree work that fills the central area and surrounds the outside of each stroke (Figure 19). In general, such letters have an angular, Gothic shape. Gothic letters can also be used for an alphabet decorated with flourishes, in which each letter has a face worked into its design. A few of these letters are shown in Figure 20.

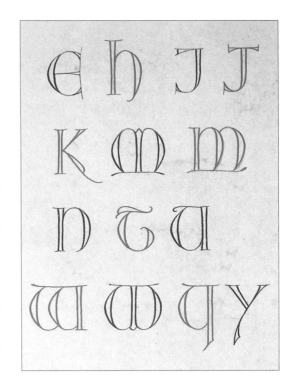

Figure 14: Rounded versions of versals are frequently used for illuminated initials.

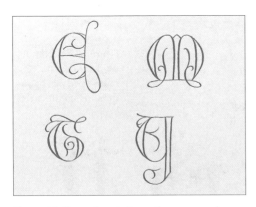

Figure 15: Curved variations of some versal letters lend themselves to floral decoration.

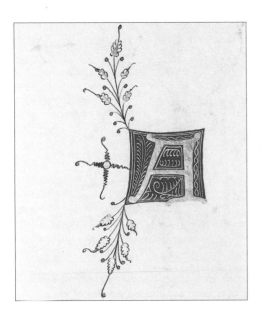

Figure 16: An illuminated letter 'A' from Lydgate's *Life of St Edmund*.

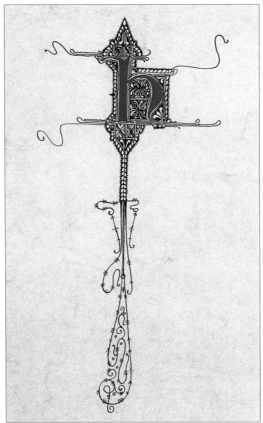

Figure 17: A letter 'H' dating from about 1330.

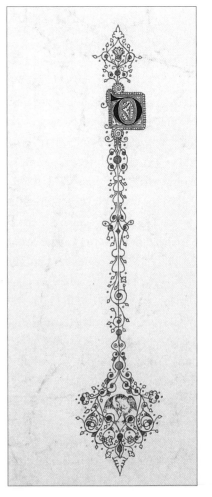

Figure 18: A letter 'D' dating from about 1480.

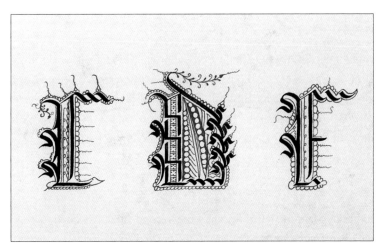

Figure 19: Letters taken from a scribe's specimen sheet dated 1447.

Figure 20: This set of Gothic letters incorporate grotesque faces.

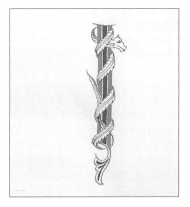

Figure 23: A pen-formed letter 'I' incorporating a serpent.

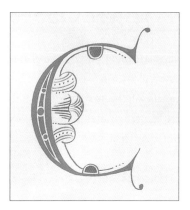

Figure 24: A simple pen-formed 'C' with light illumination.

A slightly heavier form of pen-made letter is illustrated by the 'P' in Figure 21. It is taken from a late twelfth-century manuscript that was created at Kirkstead Abbey (and is now in the British Library) by monks of the Cistercian order. The letters have not been embellished with gold, which was not permitted in their books. Similar letters are found in the Winchester Bible, which dates from the same period: the 'T' in Figure 22, for example, which is taken from folio 197v, has been worked in blue and green paint with a pen. A pen-worked serpent can be seen coiling its way up a letter 'I' (Figure 23) in folio 434v of the same manuscript. The letter 'C' that is illustrated in Figure 24 is based on a mid-twelfth-century manuscript from Reading Abbey, which is now at the Newberry Library, Chicago. Another example appears in the form of a letter 'D' that is taken from a psalter that was created at Reading Abbey in about 1160 (Figure 25) and is now at the Bodleian Library, Oxford. Contained within the letter's strokes is the Latin text *Iohes me fecit Rogerio* ('John made me for Roger'), and it was common practice for a scribe to identify himself by adding some such sort of decoration or marginal lettering to his text.

Figure 21: A pen-formed letter 'P'.

Figure 22: A pen-formed letter 'T' from the Winchester Bible.

Figure 25: A letter 'D' with accompanying glossed text.

THE GLOSS

This last-mentioned piece also incorporates another subject of interest: a gloss. Also known as a glossary, a gloss is an addition to part, or all, of the text made in either another language or as a set of explanatory notes. The gloss, which was usually written in a smaller lettering size, generally appeared underneath the main text, but sometimes also to the side or in the margin. Some great works are a complete gloss of the Bible, in which study notes have been placed alongside the relevant biblical sections. The notes frequently occupied more space than the text itself, thereby making a very large volume, such as Peter Lombard's Great Gloss on the Psalms.

PROJECT: *Creating a glossed text*

This project shows the construction of a piece of lettering with a gloss written in Welsh. The principal lettering is blackletter, and the smaller, glossed text is written in the Carolingian hand to create a contrast. The main initial letter incorporates an illustration based on the text, while the initial letter of the second verse has been enlarged and given pen-flourished decoration to fill the left-hand border.

1 Write out the blackletter text in the required size on layout paper and then repeat the process for the smaller Carolingian lettering. Compare the two sizes of lettering and decide how much space will be needed between each set of writing lines. Carolingian letters have long ascenders and descenders, so the space allowed should be sufficient to accommodate these.

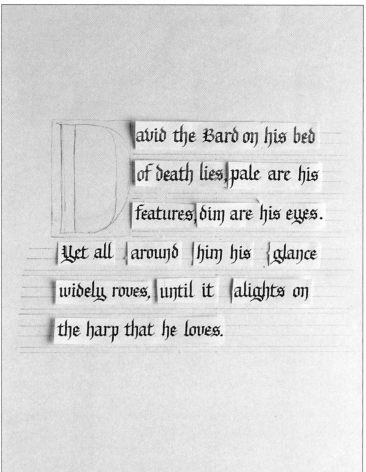

2 Start laying out the piece by roughly sketching the size and position of the initial letter on a large layout sheet (this can be altered later if necessary). Next, mark and rule guidelines for the sets of writing lines for the first verse of the text in both lettering sizes.

3 Cut the blackletter text into strips and arrange the words so that you end up with a neat block of text with lines of roughly similar length. (Leave the Carolingian-text lines empty at this stage – they will be added to the draft later.) The lines of text to the right of the initial will be shorter than those that run underneath it, starting from its left-hand edge. Place the first few strips of blackletter text in position, breaking the words at suitable points to give lines of as equal a length as possible. .

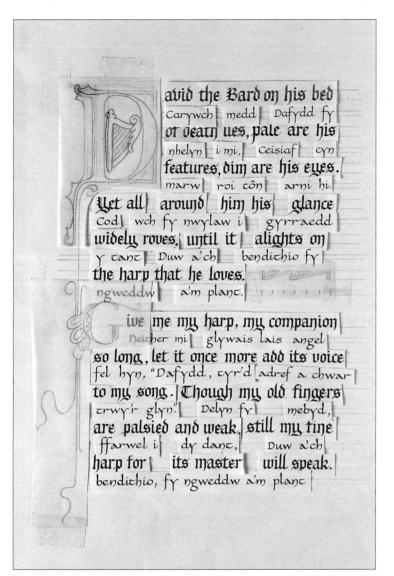

avid the Bard on his bed
of death lies, pale are his
features, dim are his eyes.
Yet all around him his glance
widely roves, until it alights on
the harp that he loves.

ive me my harp, my companion
so long, let it once more add its voice
to my song. Though my old fingers
are palsied and weak, still my fine
harp for its master will speak.

5 Write out the lettering on your chosen surface, in this instance Waterford paper (widely available from art shops).

4 Having plotted out the first verse of the large text, cut up and add the smaller text as before. Note that this text will have to be very widely spaced so that it matches the words above. Sketch in the enlarged initial letter for the second verse to determine where you will need to start the first writing line of the second verse. Rule up further writing lines for both lettering sizes and cut and paste the rest of the text in the same manner as for the first verse. If you find that you have space left at the end of either verse, you can use line-fillers to fill the gaps. With the text having been drafted, the initials can now be designed. The 'D' of David contains a simple drawing of David's harp to illustrate the text, and the penwork around the 'G' of the second verse can be worked into the tail decoration of the 'D'.

avid the Bard on his bed
Cariwch medd Dafydd fy
of death lies, pale are his
nhelyn i mi, Ceisiaf cyn
features, dim are his eyes.
marw roi tôn arni hi.
Yet all around him his glance
Cod wch fy nwylaw i gyrraedd
widely roves, until it alights on
y cant, Duw a'ch bendichio fy
the harp that he loves.
ngweddw a'm plant.

ive me my harp, my companion
neicher mi glywais lais angel
so long, let it once more add its voice
fel hyn, "Dafydd, cyr'd adref a chwar
to my song. Though my old fingers
crwy'r glyn." Delyn fy mebyd,
are palsied and weak, still my fine
ffarwel i dy danc, Duw a'ch
harp for its master will speak.
bendichio, fy ngweddw a'm plant.

6 Trace down the illustration of the initial letter and border. Write in the 'G' and its decoration.

avid the Bard on his bed

Cariwch medd Dafydd fy

of death lies, pale are his

nhelyn i mi, Ceisiaf cyn

features, dim are his eyes.

marw   roi tôn arni hi.

Yet all around him his glance

Cod wch fy nwylaw i gyrraedd

widely roves, until it alights on

y tant, Duw a'ch bendithio fy

the harp that he loves.

ngweddw a'm plant.

Give me my harp, my companion

Neither mi glywais lais angel

so long, let it once more add its voice

fel hyn, "Dafydd, tyr'd adref a chwar

to my song. Though my old fingers

trwy'r glyn." Delyn fy mebyd,

are palsied and weak, still my fine

ffarwel i dy dant, Duw a'ch

harp for its master will speak.

bendithio, fy ngweddw a'm plant.

7 Apply the gold leaf to the work. Because colours have been used for the
text, when working on the gilded areas take care that no loose gold leaf
comes into contact with the paint, to which it will probably stick. It is best
carefully to cover over all of those parts of the work that you do not need to
see with guard sheets Paint the rest of the initial letter to complete the work.

Chapter 6

Illuminated initials were used to decorate various music-related books of the Middle Ages and early Renaissance. Almost all were religious manuscripts that contained the rites, observances and procedures of public worship (the liturgy, the principal parts of which are the mass and the divine office) with musical components. All have names that you will come across when looking at old manuscripts, but which most of us are unfamiliar with today, and the main books are the antiphonal, breviary, gradual, hymnal, kyriale, missal, sacramentary and troper. Each contains particular portions of the liturgy, some of which will be described in further detail below.

MUSIC BOOKS

THE GRADUAL AND KYRIALE

The gradual – the principal choir book used during the mass – is one of the most common music books dating from this period. Because all of the monastery's monks would gather round to read it on the lectern, the books themselves were very large. The first sung parts of the mass were often introduced by beautifully worked illuminated initials that could measure as much as 25–30cm (nearly 10–12") across.

Figure 1: A letter 'B', from a fourteenth-century gradual, in outline with gold paint added.

Figure 2: The background colours are added.

Figures 1–4 shows a 'B' taken from a fourteenth-century gradual that is today owned by the Biblioteka Jagiellonska, Cracow, Poland. The historiated letter is fairly simple, having just a few embellishing curls and flourishes, with an attractive crossing-over of the two central curves of the 'B', the ends of which then curve around the first upright stroke with floral terminations.

The letter is enclosed by a straight-sided rectangle, the ends of the first upright stroke of the 'B' then being worked into attractive, floral curls that sprout out of the enclosing box and into the margin. The central scene is neatly arranged, with the head of the figure appearing almost centrally in the top bowl of the 'B', and the arm and raised spear sited in a very eye-catching position. The dragon in the lower part of the letter has been carefully worked into the available space, and its coiled tail flows out of the bordering frame into the margin.

The kyriale contains the ordinary chants of the mass, which remain unchanged throughout the ecclesiastical year. Although the kyriale was usually incorporated into the gradual, it sometimes formed a separate volume during the late Middle Ages.

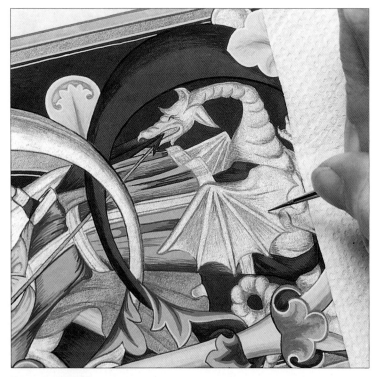

Figure 3: Modelling is added to the base colours.

Figure 4: The finished letter.

PROJECT: *Creating an illuminated letter for a gradual*

The illuminated letter 'E' in Figure 5 comes at the beginning of a Dominican gradual dating from late fifteenth-century northern Italy. It measures 56.5 x 40.5cm (22 x 16") and is now at the Victoria & Albert Museum in London. This letter is of a slightly later date than those that we have studied so far, and is Renaissance in style. The central decoration is much more naturalistic than that found in the more stylised, Gothic letters. The outer surround of the letter is a solid area of flat gold leaf and a typical biblical scene is depicted in the centre. One of the main differences between this style of painting and Gothic illustration is that the figures and features of the picture are not outlined. The 'E' itself is a strongly designed letter, with its laurel wreaths and scrolling acanthus leaves giving it a weight and formality that contrasts with the illustration that it frames.

Figure 5: A fifteenth-century gradual contains the original of this letter 'E'.

1 Make a drawing of the letter and trace down the outline onto vellum. Apply the flat gold leaf to the corners. You could use either transfer gold or loose gold leaf on a base of gold size.

2 Paint in the background colours. Remember that in order to paint this softer type of decoration successfully, you will need to create many layers of modelling, beginning with darker shades of each colour to define the shapes.

3 Use the dry-brushwork technique to achieve a graduating effect from light to dark. This technique involves loading the brush with a minimal amount of paint so that a hazy effect, rather than a solid line, is created by each brushstroke. This also enables you to blend the colours well. Add lighter colours to highlight particular areas, in this case to give the effect of light falling on the left side of the robe and haloes.

MUSICAL NOTATION

During the mid-eleventh century, when musical notation first began to appear in manuscripts, musical notes were not written as we know them today. A simpler system of notes, known as neumes, was used instead, the neumes being written above the text to indicate the rise and fall, or repetition of pitch, of the melody. Various different, regional systems of neumes having been identified, it seems that no single, regular series of symbols was in use.

The neumes were written on staves of four lines rather than the five that we now use. The staves were often drawn in red, while the neumes were usually written in black ink. Draw the staves with a ruling pen, taking care to keep the ink flowing steadily along the whole length of the line (Figure 6). Alternatively, you could use a mapping pen and rule; although the results are less precise than those produced with a ruling pen, this effect can sometimes be more pleasing, as most musical staves on old manuscripts were not perfectly straight (Figure 7). In addition, vellum buckles when it becomes warm, which can also distort the work, giving the appearance of slightly crooked lines. Music pens are available that draw a five-lined stave in one stroke, but note that you are confined to a single size of nib that draws a stave of about 10mm (⅜") in width and that it is also quite difficult to make the ink flow continuously from all five points for any length of time.

Figure 6: Music staves drawn with a ruling pen.

Figure 7: Music staves drawn with a mapping pen.

In order to indicate the pitch of the notes to be sung, a clef symbol should be placed on the relevant stave line, identifying notes placed on that line as either a 'c' (Figure 8) or an 'f' (Figure 9). The other notes are then pitched in accordance with this indicated note. Our modern treble- and base-clef symbols are a little more complex (Figure 10). Remember that no time signatures or bar lines were used, and that where vertical lines divide the stave into sections this was done to match the notes with the text below.

Figure 8: The 'c' clef used in medieval music manuscripts.

Figure 9" The 'f' clef found in medieval manuscripts.

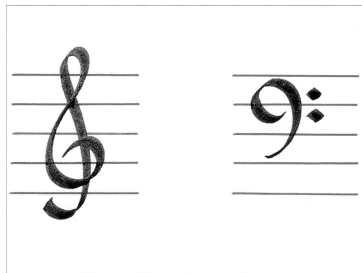

Figure 10: Modern treble and bass clefs.

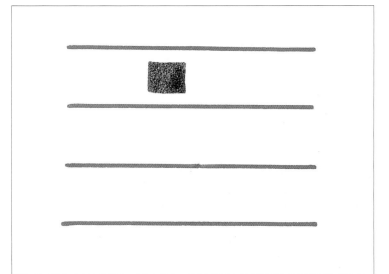

Figure 11: Music notes.

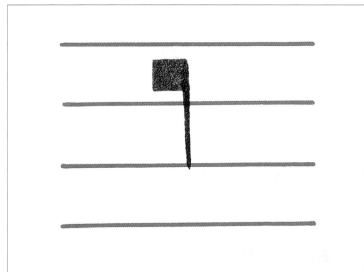

Figure 12: Tails to notes.

You will need a large-sized nib to write the notes themselves, which is used with the edge held vertically to make a stroke the full width of the nib (Figure 11). The stroke should occupy at least half of the space between the stave lines. Tails were sometimes given to the notes by means of a very thin line that was made by drawing the pen straight downwards (Figure 12). Notes were also occasionally joined together to make a diagonal stroke over several stave lines (Figure

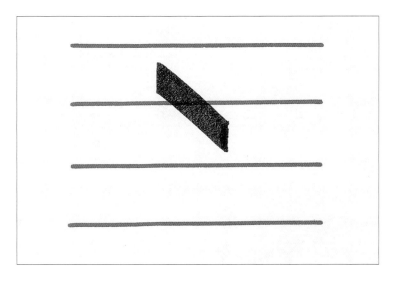

Figure 13: Notes joined together.

ROTUNDA LETTERING

The rotunda lettering style, which was used for many musical manuscripts, is large, bold and written with the pen held at an extremely shallow angle. Indeed, some of the strokes are made with the nib held at an almost horizontal angle to the page (Figure 14). The ascending and descending strokes are very short, and the hand comprises a strongly contrasting combination of thick and thin strokes, some of the connecting strokes being so thin that they are sometimes barely visible.

In the rotunda alphabet, the letter 'i' was frequently either left undotted or was given a very thin, diagonal stroke. Containing as it does a great many similar-looking, upright strokes, the hand is difficult to read, but because the letters were very large and the songs that they spelled out were also probably well known to the singers, this was presumably not a problem. The medieval reader would furthermore have been much more familiar with the lettering style and therefore able to decipher it more quickly than the modern reader.

The letters illustrated in Figure 14, which have been written between writing lines 18mm (¾") apart, are on the scale that you will find in many graduals. The width of the nib used was 4mm (⁵⁄₁₆"), which corresponds to a size L14 in the William Mitchell poster-pen series, which is recommended for large-sized lettering. Because most large nibs do not have the sharp edge that is required for fine lettering, it may be necessary to sharpen your nib with an oil stone (a small, very fine, grinding stone that can be purchased from hardware shops). Using a fairly light touch, draw the nib across the stone three

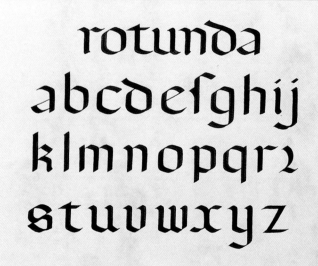

Figure 14: Rotunda lettering.

or four times in the direction shown in Figure 15. Draw the nib along the stone on its reverse side (Figure 16) once, and then very lightly along the corners, which should remove any burr or rough edges. Try writing a few strokes to make sure that the sharpened edge is even and that the strokes that the nib produces are crisp. Although it takes practice to sharpen nibs well, and you may spoil a few before perfecting the technique, it is very useful to be able to sharpen nibs when they lose their accuracy.

Figure 15: Sharpening a nib on an oil stone.

Figure 16: Draw the back of the nib, then the corners, across the stone to finish.

Planning a musical manuscript

When planning a song sheet or music book, remember that you will need to write the words first, as they take up more space than the notes. The notes should then be placed in their relevant positions on the stave lines so that they tie in with the words.

Figure 17: A song sheet – draft.

Figure 18: The initial letter with a flat gold-leaf centre and border complemented by strong colours.

Figure 19: Song sheet – finished.

In order to make a truly medieval-style musical manuscript, the size of the page should be large, and the example shown in figures 17–19 is 55 x 40cm (21 x 15 ¾"). The page's outer margin is usually double the width of the inner margin, the edge of which is bound into the book. The two central margins of a double-page spread will together measure the same width as the outer margins. A fifth of the width of the whole page, in this case 8cm (3 ²/₁₆"), is used for the outer margin and a tenth of the width for the inner margin. If you plan to make a manuscript book that has several pages, and most songs take up more than one page, you will need to plan the work in terms of double-page spreads, allowing the correct margin width in the centre for both sides (Figure 20).

Figure 20: Page plan, margins.

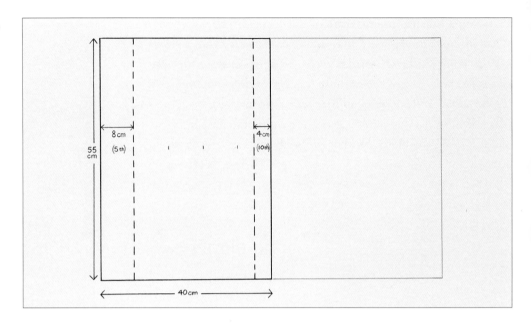

THE SACRAMENTARY, MISSAL, ANTIPHONAL, HYMNAL, BREVIARY AND TROPER

Another type of musical service book, called the sacramentary, contained the prayers that were recited by the celebrant during the mass (the other parts of the mass were contained in the gradual and other books, such as the evangelary or epistolery).

A missal was a fuller service book that contained chants, prayers and readings, as well as the ceremonial directions that were used by the priest for the performance of the mass. The missal was introduced during the Carolingian period, and because it combined the various parts required for the mass, had supplanted the sacramentary by the late thirteenth century. The 'D' in Figure 18 on page 100 was part of a missal, as was the 'T' in Figure 14 on page 97.

The book that contained the sung parts of the divine office is called the antiphonal. Like the gradual, because it was used by the choir, it was large in format. The antiphonal contained historiated initials that highlighted the principal events of the liturgical year. (Hymns were usually, but not always, contained in a separate book.)

Figure 21: A letter 'A' from an antiphonal.

Although manuscript vellum is designed for writing on both sides, the hair side is slightly preferable to the flesh side. You can tell which side is which because the hair side – the side that faced outwards on the animal – is smoother and the veins are less prominent (Figure 22). The flesh side is a little rougher – especially the corners of the skin, which frequently reveal knife cuts in the thicker areas – and is also slightly more absorbent . Use the hair side for the front page.

If you are using more than four pages, it is usual to plan the manuscript so that hair side faces hair side and flesh side faces flesh side when the sheets are put together.

Figure 22: Hair and flesh sides of vellum. The 'hair' is on the back, while the 'flesh' is on the front of the sheet.

PROJECT: *Creating a letter from an antiphonal*

Figure 21 shows an initial 'A', taken from a late thirteenth-century Italian antiphonal, whose central scene depicts Christ enthroned.

The size of the manuscript is 582 x 402mm (23 x 15 ¾"), and it is housed at the J Paul Getty Museum in California.

1 The vibrant blue of this letter, which contrasts with the raised gold leaf and small areas of brilliant red, make it very eye-catching. The illumination is delicate, the pale-blue strapwork at each end of the final stroke of the 'A' being quite lightweight.

2 The small floral motifs that are scattered over the outer area of ultramarine are intricately worked, as are the hairline red and pale-blue lines around the outer edges. The vibrancy of the colours, however, give this initial great strength.

PROJECT: *Creating a letter from a hymnal*

The hymnal contained the hymns that were sung during the divine office, which were arranged according to the liturgical year. Although it could form a separate section in an antiphonal or psalter (a book of the psalms), its contents eventually became part of the breviary (described below).

Figure 23 shows a reconstruction of an historiated initial 'A' from a hymnal. Its construction partly consists of the body of a dragon, which arches up the left-hand side and over the top of the letter. The whole outer decoration of the page comprises a border of matching scrollwork that contains many small figures and faces hidden within the illumination. The style is looser than that of the carefully constructed 'A' of the antiphonal described above.

Figure 23: This letter 'A', from a hymnal, is formed by an arching dragon.

1 The outline of the letter is traced onto the vellum.

2 Gold is applied to the traced outline.

3 The background colours are painted.

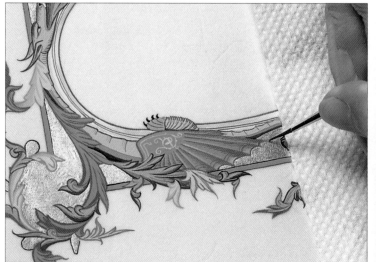

4 The shapes are outlined, then modelling is added.

Dating from the eleventh century, the breviary was a service book that was made up of a collection of other books to comprise the whole text for the celebration of the divine office. The accompanying illuminated initials often contained biblical scenes or scenes depicting the performance of the divine office. The breviary was originally used only by monks, and all members of monastic orders were committed to its daily recitation. The letter 'B' in Figure 18 on page 111 is taken from a sixteenth-century French breviary.

Another way of adding musical notes to a text is by using tropes, notes placed above the words to be sung, thereby roughly indicating the rise and fall in pitch required. Because no music staves are used, they only give the reader minimal musical assistance. The lines between some of the notes and words are furthermore not bar lines, but instead indicate the corresponding sections of words and notes. Tropers (Figure 24) were books that contained this sort of notation – which was added to the chants of the mass or divine office – that appeared from the early Middle Ages onwards.

Although early transcripts of non-religious music are difficult to find, collections of troubadours' songs dating from the mid-thirteenth century onwards survive. We will conclude this chapter with a small piece of modern music, which has an illuminated initial (figures 25–26).

Figure 25: An illuminated piece of music.

Figure 26: Detail of the initial letter.

Figure 24: An example of a page from a troper.

Chapter 7

Beautiful borders add so much to the illuminated page, and a variety of styles will be considered in this chapter, along with their accompanying initial letters and lettering styles.

ILLUMINATED BORDERS

PROJECT: *Types of border*

1 Some borders evolve naturally from the gradual increase in embellishment of the illuminated letter.

2 To begin with, a little extra ornamentation is added to the outer edges or corners of the letter.

3 Then the centre is filled and more embellishment is given to the outer branches.

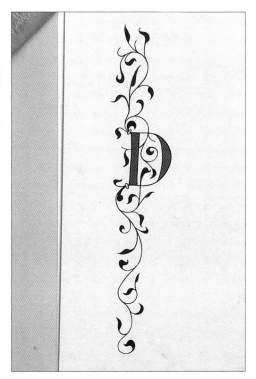

4 The branches are made to creep further and further outward, along the left margin.

5 Then decoration is taken along the top border.

6 Finally, all four sides are decorated, so that a full-scale border surrounds the whole page.

Our first few examples are based on borders found in the *Très Riches Heures of Jean, Duc du Berry* (which is today in the Musée Condé at Chantilly, France), which contains many stunning pages of rich illumination. The book was made during the fifteenth century by several different artists, and was not completed and bound until some years after the duke's death. Each page measures 29 x 21 cm (11 $^7/_{16}$ x 8") and is full of miniature paintings, initials and ornate borders.

Figure 1 shows an initial 'D' from folio 60v, part of a large, illuminated page depicting the coronation of the Virgin Mary. The floral shoots that spring from each corner of the letter emerge from a pink flower, after which alternating shoots of different colours curl back and forth to form the whole pattern. The colours are very bright and the modelling is light and simple, with a little shading and highlighting giving a three-dimensional effect. Large gold seeds also protrude from each corner shoot. The shield in the centre of the letter contains the armorial bearings of France.

Another letter of a similar style, but with a different colour scheme, is shown in Figure 2. It is taken from a page depicting St John on Patmos (folio17v). The large blue, pink and cream flowers are interspersed with small gold stars or seed heads. The decoration again springs naturally from the corner points of the letter 'I' and flows along the border for the length required to balance the other decoration and lettering on the page.

If you are working on a letter that does not have a convenient corner to develop into border, you will need to make a shoot 'grow' from some point along the edge of the letter and then work it into a border in the same way as for other letters (Figure 3). Remember not to add shoots to areas which could result in the letter looking like another one. For example, a shoot emerging from the bottom-right corner of an 'O' could make it look like a 'Q'.

Figure 1: This simple border springs from a letter 'D' enclosing a shield.

Figure 3: Extra shoots can be added to the rim of a letter.

Figure 2: A letter 'I' with a border in an unusual colour scheme.

PROJECT: *Reconstructing a border*

A more complex border can be seen sprouting from a letter 'K' on a double-page spread (folios 71 and 72) that depicts the procession of St Gregory (Figure 4). The letter leads into a beautifully coloured, scrolling border that flows along the left and top margins of the page. This design can be easily adapted for use on any other piece of lettering by means of lengthening or shortening the floral work, and we will therefore break down this border to see how it is constructed.

Figure 4: A letter 'K' with an elaborate two-sided border.

| The ascending stroke of the initial 'K' has a green stem running up the centre, which is the starting point for all of the branches.

2 The branches issue from three points on this stem, each beginning with an opening flower. The shoots forming the border grow out of each flower in various directions. Those for the left-hand border issue from the bottom corner of the 'K', and then the top-left portion peels off from the flower head at the top of the 'K'. The top-right branches emanate from a flower head part of the way up the ascending stroke of the letter.

3 Each of the branches is a continuation of the main green stem inside the 'K'. As the foliage branches out, each piece is reversed back and forth to give a change of colour and direction.

4 After the green stems, blue, red or pink branches are introduced.

5 Here and there a flower is added.

6 Small groups of golden seeds are used to fill the remaining gaps.

The gold background of the 'K' is scattered with a trellis of small, alternating, pink and blue flowers, which gives weight to the letter which might otherwise be overpowered by the complexity and depth of the border. You cannot paint over gold leaf very successfully because it is too resistant to gouache paint; although the paint may seem to stick at first if extra gum is added, it will eventually flake, or be rubbed, off. The small flowers on the gold background were therefore painted into the blank spaces that were left for them when the gilding was carried out.

Bastarda lettering

The lettering in the *Très Riches Heures* is written in a neat, Gothic style (Figure 5) that indicates a slightly cursive slant. This hand represents a shift away from the upright styles that were previously used towards the lettering style known as bastarda, or *batarde bourguignonne*. As its name suggests, bastarda lettering is something of a hybrid amalgamation of two other styles: although the letters are basically of a Gothic nature, their forward slant is characteristic of the italic styles that would follow. Bastarda letters are very decorative and were used in the production of many beautiful works.

As with most lettering styles, when you look through reference books on calligraphy, you will see an array of different scripts that are loosely described as bastarda. Indeed, there are so many variations on the general theme that it is difficult to identify any single alphabet of letters as representing the definitive bastarda hand. The alphabet shown in Figure 6 is based on the bastarda lettering that appears on a grant of arms dated 1492 (which can be seen in the Victoria & Albert Museum under the reference MS L 4362-1948).

Figure 5: The lettering style used in the *Très Riches Heures*.

Figure 6: Bastarda lettering.

The most distinctive feature of this hand is the vertical 's'. Although it takes a while for the modern eye to become accustomed to reading the text, as well as to replacing the familiar 's' in the mind's eye with the stroke shown, bastarda is essentially a clear, well-defined style, unlike the many Gothic hands that preceded it that contained too many upright strokes. The deep, curving serif on the upright strokes was developed into a feature by some artists (Figure 7), who would bring the point down to the top writing line using a fine hairline. Bastarda was not used for official church-service books, the more established scripts produced by monks of earlier periods instead continuing to be favoured for such works.

Figure 7: Extended serifs sometimes used with bastarda letters.

Foliate-bar borders

Borders around three sides of the text became very popular, and figures 8–11 show examples, all of which illustrate the texts of the English author Geoffrey Chaucer.

The first (Figure 8) is dated about 1450, and can today be seen at Glasgow University Library. It illustrates Chaucer's *Romaunt de la Rose*, a translation into Middle English verse of the French *Roman de la Rose* ('The Romance of the Rose'), a very popular medieval text. Although the original illumination work was quite crude, the design of the border is very attractive. The initial letter sits within the block of text and is attached to a bar running along the height of the page. The bar is split, with a coloured band on the letter side and a gold band on the side nearest the margin. The coloured band leads from the letter, with pink being used at the top and blue at the bottom, into the corner pieces, which are composed of leaves and large, lily-like flowers. The large leaves, which are painted in various colours, sprout from the coloured bar. The effect of a gold background in the corner blocks is achieved by filling the space between each leaf with a portion of gold outlined with ink. The top and bottom borders are formed with thin, pen-drawn fronds that terminate in single flowers and leaves. Smaller leaves and seeds, which are painted in green or gold, are drawn along the length of these fronds. The accompanying English text is written in the bastarda hand.

The second example (Figure 9), which is today housed at Lichfield Cathedral, also dates from the mid-fifteenth century and was probably made in London. It depicts the opening of 'The Miller's Tale', from Chaucer's *Canterbury Tales*. The fine sprays of foliage sprouting from the gold-and-blue bar border frame an attractive, bastarda text with an illuminated initial 'W'. Although it conforms to the same basic theme of a letter attached to a bar, the treatment of the border is quite different – in terms of both weight and general appearance – from the first example discussed above. To begin with, the gold background of the letter, rather than shoots

Figure 8: A foliate-bar border with initial 'T'.

Figure 9: A foliate-bar border with initial 'W'.

Figure 10: Another border with an initial 'W', in a more evenly spaced design.

sprouting from the letter itself, attaches the letter to the gold of the bar. The blue-coloured section of the bar furthermore emerges from behind the letter rather than branching out from its corners. The large leaves have serrated edges and cross over the gold bar to form the starting points for the finer details in the border. The sprays of fine-lined seeds and small flower heads, which are all drawn in fairly tight, single coils, are well spaced along the length of the border. Each small seed head consists of a looped shape filled with green paint, although some of the leaves and seed heads are highlighted with raised gold. Tiny sprinklings of raised gold in borders of this sort can be very attractive, and have just as much of a decorative effect as larger areas of gold. Note the very angular styling of the small gold leaves to form oblong shapes.

The final example (figures 10–11) of this set is another rendition of a 'W' from 'The Miller's Tale', dating from about 1440. This, along with another page from the same work, is in the John Rylands Library in Manchester, while 11 further leaves from the same manu-

Figure 11: Detail from the 'W' in Figure 10.

script are in the Rosenbach Foundation Museum in Philadelphia. The 'W' is drawn in a similar manner to the version discussed above, but the floral sprays are more regular and continuous along each portion of the border, with the seed heads and flowers being set at approximately equal distances around the border. The fine lines of the many leaves and seeds (which are best drawn with a mapping pen) form quite a dense covering, giving an interesting texture. The flowers and corner pieces are painted in rather muted colours, which have probably dulled quite a lot over time. Indeed, the gold work on the original manuscript has deteriorated a great deal, with the gesso base showing through in many places, which is a great shame, as the decoration is very accurately painted. The text occupied the bottom half of the area within the border, commencing from the 'W'. The top half of the border surrounds a simple illustration of the miller on his steed.

A fine, illuminated 'T', taken from a mid-fifteenth-century missal from Ghent, is the starting point for the top and bottom borders made up of small and intricate foliate work shown in figures 12–14. With its terminating leaves to each exterior loop, the central fretwork pattern inside the 'T' is quite unusual. Similar leaves appear in the border, principally in the top and bottom margins of the page, linked by a bar that sprouts a few additional leaves. Two or three different flower and leaf shapes make up the border design (Figure 15), which is a simple series of coils alternating from side to side, with a flower in the centre of each coil and another in each large gap above and below. The smaller gaps have been filled with seed heads and leaves, the artist having used a looped or twisted shape for some of the seed heads (Figure16).

Figure 12: Draw the outline of the border.

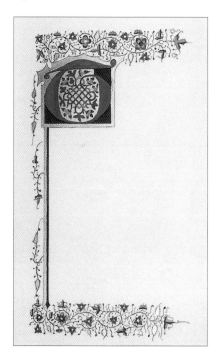

Figure 13: Trace the design onto vellum, outline in ink, then paint the background colours.

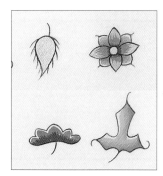

Figure 15: Flower and leaf shapes forming the border.

Figure 16: Twisted seed shapes.

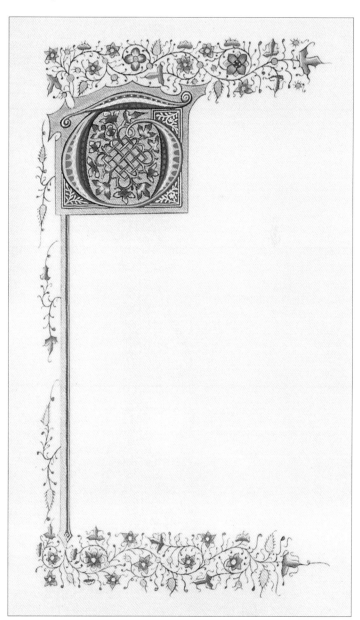

Figure 14: Add shading and highlighting to complete the border.

Figure 17: This initial letter 'D' with a bar border is based on folio 29 of the Grey-FitzPayn Hours. Many small animals have been incorporated into the design, which i s also rich in diaper patterns.

PROJECT: *Creating a vine-leaf border*

A type of foliate-bar border that is frequently seen in fourteenth-century manuscripts is shown in Figure 18. (This example is based on folio 242r from the St Denis Missal, at the Victoria and Albert Museum, size 235mm x 170mm). An illuminated letter on the left-hand side is the starting point, from which a fairly straight-sided bar border extends to form the main framework of the page. Stylised vine leaves are the basis of the decoration that springs from the corners and runs along the outer edges of the frame.

Not only is vine-leaf decoration very attractive, but it is also easy to reproduce. The border runs right round the page and often contains a central dividing line that breaks the text into two columns. The bars are heavier than those that we have looked at so far, with deeper, patterned strips (similar to some of the line-fillers that we discussed in earlier chapters) being used for the coloured portions of the bars. The corners are worked with curling branches and arching points to form a link between the top and side bars.

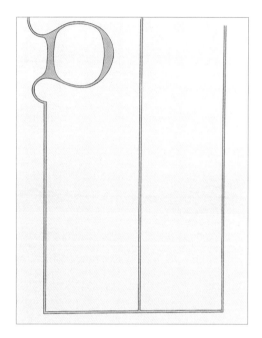

1 To form the vine-leaf border, first run the bar lines from the corners of the initial letter around each margin.

2 Form the main stem of each piece of foliage by making an elongated 's' shape branching off from the bar line either at the ends or at any suitable points in the centre of the line to fill the required space.

Figure 18: A typical vine-leaf border.

3 The basic vine-leaf shape.

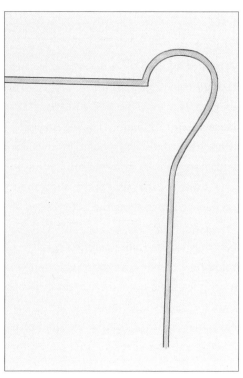

4 This leaf is spaced at regular intervals along the stem, alternating with a blunt stub. Each leaf follows the natural direction of growth of the branch.

5 Smaller, half-grown leaves are sometimes drawn at the beginning of branches, and these can also be useful for filling spaces in your design into which a large leaf will not fit.

6 Carry out the corners of the bar line in a rounded sweep.

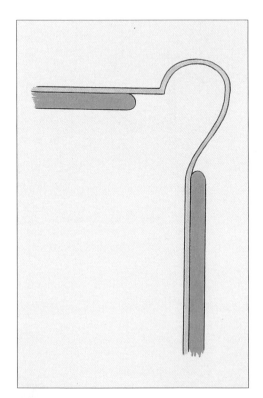

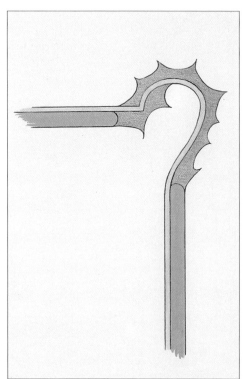

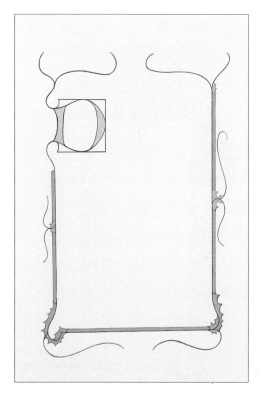

7 Draw strips of colour along each side, making them slightly wider than the main bar.

8 Next, fill the areas in the corners that link these strips with a series of pointed curves. These areas are worked in gold and are drawn either on the outside or on both sides of the bar.

9 Although the bar is not usually continued around the top border, the vine stems fill this area, branching out to the left and right of the bars.

10 The whole border design is drawn, then traced into place on the vellum. The gold areas are painted with gold powder.

11 The vine leaves are painted in deepening shades of blue and red, then finished with a lighter highlighting colour.

12 The initial letter is painted with a diapered background and lightly modelled figures.

Rinceaux

The vine-leaf border was taken to complex extremes in some later Renaissance manuscripts. Indeed, the close mesh of leaves and flowers spaced evenly over a four-sided and very wide border totally dominated the accompanying text. Decoration of this type is known as rinceaux.

Figure 19 shows a section of an intricate rinceaux border of close-set vine leaves arranged in tightly curling stems that completely cover the border area.

Figure 19: Rinceaux.

Chapter 8

Markedly different Renaissance styles of illumination followed the medieval Gothic. Renaissance is the French word for 'rebirth', and from the mid-fourteenth to mid-sixteenth centuries the manuscript painting of the Renaissance period saw a revival of the classical styles of antiquity in the work of artists who became known as humanists. We will look at three distinct illumination styles from this period: white-vine stem, humanist antiqua and trompe l'oeil.

RENAISSANCE ILLUMINATION

THE WHITE-VINE-STEM STYLE

Figure 1: A letter 'C' from an Italian model book dated *circa* 1200.

Figure 2: White-vine-stem construction.

Humanism – whose aim was to revive classical learning – developed in late fourteenth-century Florence and was an important component of the Renaissance for the illuminator. The humanist script was developed by such great Florentine classicists as Niccolo Niccoli and Poggio Bracciolini, the Gothic scripts having been considered too difficult to read, too small and too full of abbreviations. Florence and Rome were the leaders in humanist book production.

As the fifteenth century dawned in Florence, a type of illumination known as white-vine stem, or *bianchi girari*, developed (Figure 1), one of the earliest surviving Florentine examples of which dates from 1408. Although the Italian humanists were attempting to emulate what they believed to be the antique texts of Greece and Rome, they were, in fact, using twelfth-century Italian manuscripts as their models that dated from no later than Carolingian times. (Perhaps they thought that the interweaving white-vine stems were based on the acanthus foliage that is found on Roman marble columns.) A letter 'C' taken from an Italian model book of initials dated about 1200, which is shown in Figure 1, is clearly a model for the white-vine-stemwork of the Renaissance. Whatever its origins, however, the style became a very popular accompaniment to humanist texts and quickly spread northwards throughout Europe during the early fifteenth century.

PROJECT: *Creating a white-vine-stem letter*

The initial shown in Figure 3 is based on a letter 'F' taken from a Florentine manuscript dating from between about 1460 and 1470. (The original manuscript is at the Österreichische Nationalbibliothek in Vienna and another volume from the same set can be seen in the Spencer Collection in the New York Public Library.) The letter is accompanied by a text written in humanist script, and a border in the same style appears on three sides of the manuscript. The work is signed by the scribe Giovanni Francesco Martino.

Figure 3: A white-vine-stem letter 'F' with humanist text.

1 After writing the text, trace the drawing of the letter onto the vellum.

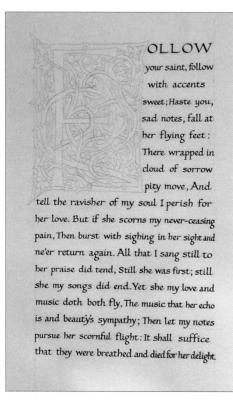

2 Gold leaf is added to the letter 'F'. The letter that was complemented by white-vine-stemwork was usually illuminated in gold leaf, while the white-vine parts of the design comprised a fairly simple trellis of curling stems branching off at intervals to form either small, unadorned shoots or floral and foliate terminations.

3 The branches are outlined with black ink, then the red guidelines are removed.

4 The background colours are painted; they were frequently divided into blue, green and red portions.

5 The white-vine areas were either left as blank parchment or vellum or were modelled slightly with light-beige or cream-coloured paint.

6 These coloured areas are then given further embellishment in the form of small groups of three gold or white dots overpainted on the background colours.

Figure 4: A white-vine-stem 'D' based on a Florentine manuscript dated 1448.

A Florentine manuscript, dated 1448 and now housed at Balliol College, Oxford University (reference MS.78 B, f.108v), is the source of the illuminated 'D' illustrated in Figure 4. This is the only illumination on a large page of humanist text, Roman capital letters forming the rest of the title words. The letter occupies almost half of the width of the block of text and a third of its length. Apart from the two shoots of vine that spread along the left-hand border, the letter is designed within the usual squared block. The circular, gold seed heads on thin tendrils are a novel feature on this type of manuscript, however.

THE HUMANIST, HUMANIST-ANTIQUA AND CANCELLERESCA HANDS

Owing much to the Carolingian styles of lettering (Figure 5), the humanist hand was small and neat, with quite light and simple letters that had a rounded appearance. The 's' was almost invariably written in the long form illustrated. Two or three versions of some of the letters were used within the same manuscript, however, for example, an upright 'd' and a flat-topped 'd' (Figure 6), while the 'g' had several variants. The diagonally stroked letters 'v' and 'w' are sometimes hard to pick out in a Latin text, as they were usually written in the rounded form shown in Figure 5. (The capital letters with-

in the same text were written using the more recognisable diagonal strokes.) Some minuscule texts used diagonally stroked versions, however, while the 'y' was written as shown in Figure 6. The serifs tended to be fairly large and formed quite a pronounced hook at the end of ascenders and descenders (Figure 7).

The spacing between the lines of text was quite wide, between two and two-and-a-half times the height of the letters, which creates a feeling of spaciousness that contrasts with the rather dense covering and intricacy of the illuminated letters and borders.

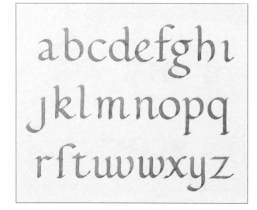

Figure 5: Humanist lettering.

Figure 6: Alternative forms of some of the humanist letters.

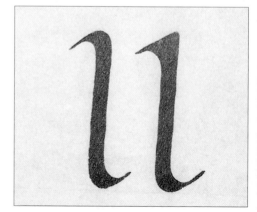

Figure 7: Serifs for humanist antiqua.

Figure 9: The design is drawn and traced onto the vellum and gold is added to the letter.

The Roman influence on Renaissance illumination appears in very formal, classical designs, such as the 'D' illustrated in Figure 8, which is taken from the Bentivoglio Hours, an Italian book of hours dating from about 1500 that is today in the Victoria & Albert Museum. A pedestal effect surrounds the letter, with lighter scroll-work at the top and bottom forming a border piece (figures 9–10). Penwork was used for the fine strokes contained within the decoration at the top and bottom. The accompanying text is written in the humanist-antiqua style.

Humanist antiqua is a much more formal style than the rounded humanist hand. The letters are written with the pen held at a very shallow angle, thereby enabling the terminations of the strokes to be squared off to make a strong stylistic reference to classical Roman roots. This stylistic reference is further underlined by the accompanying boxed initial letters and decoration that appears throughout the text.

Figure 11 shows a full alphabet of humanist-antiqua letters, based on the text of the Bentivoglio Hours. The script resembles printers' letters and could conceivably have been influenced by the printed books that were then starting to be produced. The smaller, boxed Roman capitals that appear throughout the text are usually painted letters that were constructed as illustrated in Figure 12.

An illuminated letter 'G' (Figure 13) that was used in conjunction with the humanist-antiqua script in a Florentine manuscript dated about 1522 is in the same style, albeit larger. It also has a little more embellishment in the form of a fine, white outline to the letter and finely worked, floral detail in the corners and centre of the 'G'. The 'P' shown in Figure 14, which is again in the same style as the previous examples, has a small, additional piece of decoration at the side. This letter, which is taken from a diminutive Florentine book

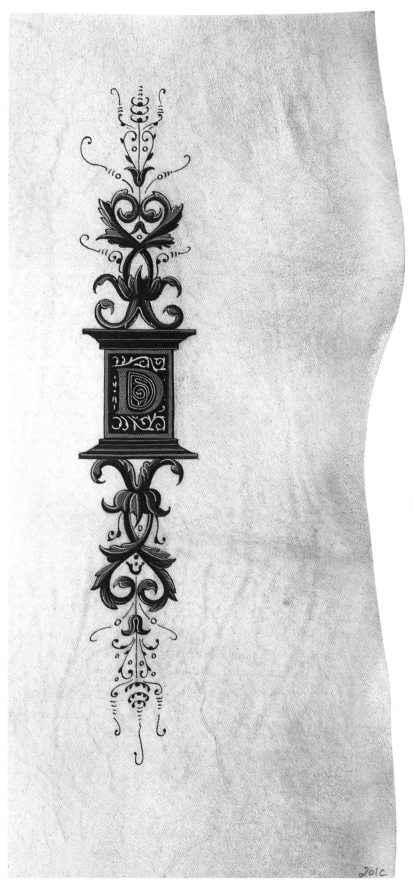

Figure 8: A letter 'D' with elongated border decoration.

Figure 10: The background colour is painted, then modelling can be applied to the decoration.

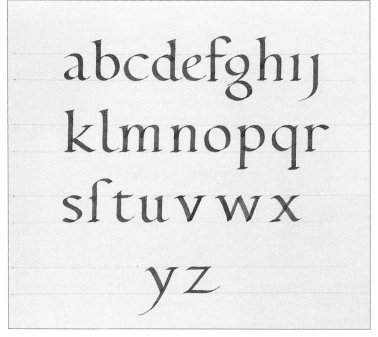

Figure 11: Humanist-antiqua lettering.

of hours dated 1540, accompanied text that was written in a script known as cancelleresca.

Cancelleresca is a slanted lettering style that was one of the forerunners of the italic hand, and the alphabet is shown in Figure 15. It is a fairly quick and uncomplicated hand to reproduce, with easy, flowing strokes. Note that the 's' was sometimes written in the long, 'f' form. The spacing between the lines of lettering was usually twice the width of the writing lines, giving a light and elegant texture to the page. Softer, floral decoration accompanied this script more often than in the case of its predecessors. Small pieces of floral and scrollwork were either used as line-fillers (Figure 16) or to make decorative patterns within the text (Figure 17). In this last example, which begins with a simple, boxed Roman 'M', the lines of text are formed into a 'V' shape to make room for the floral embellishments.

The antiqua style of illumination was carried to extremes in some very lavish pages of rich, classical ornamentation full of columns, arches, urns and trophies. Heads of Roman emperors, shields and spears were painted in strong colours. An example that can be seen in the Herzog August Bibliothek, in Wolfenbüttel, Germany, that was made for the king of Hungary between about 1485 and 1490, includes many of these features. (Most of these ornate manuscripts were produced for the book collections of rich and powerful Italian families.) In some of the more elaborate pages, the style of many of the pieces becomes very static, with heavy blocks of colour and ornamentation surrounding small pieces of text. The grotesques of medieval art were replaced by putti (naked infants, often depicted with wings), masks, vases and other classical motifs. Detailed architectural frames were furthermore built up around the page with vibrant colours and an extravagant use of gold to produce overpowering and ostentatious effects.

Figure 12: Boxed Roman capitals used with humanist-antiqua text.

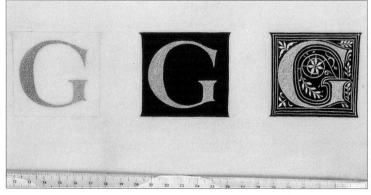

Figure 13: A letter 'G' based on a Florentine manuscript dated *circa* 1522.

Figure 14: A letter 'P' based on a Florentine book of hours dated 1540.

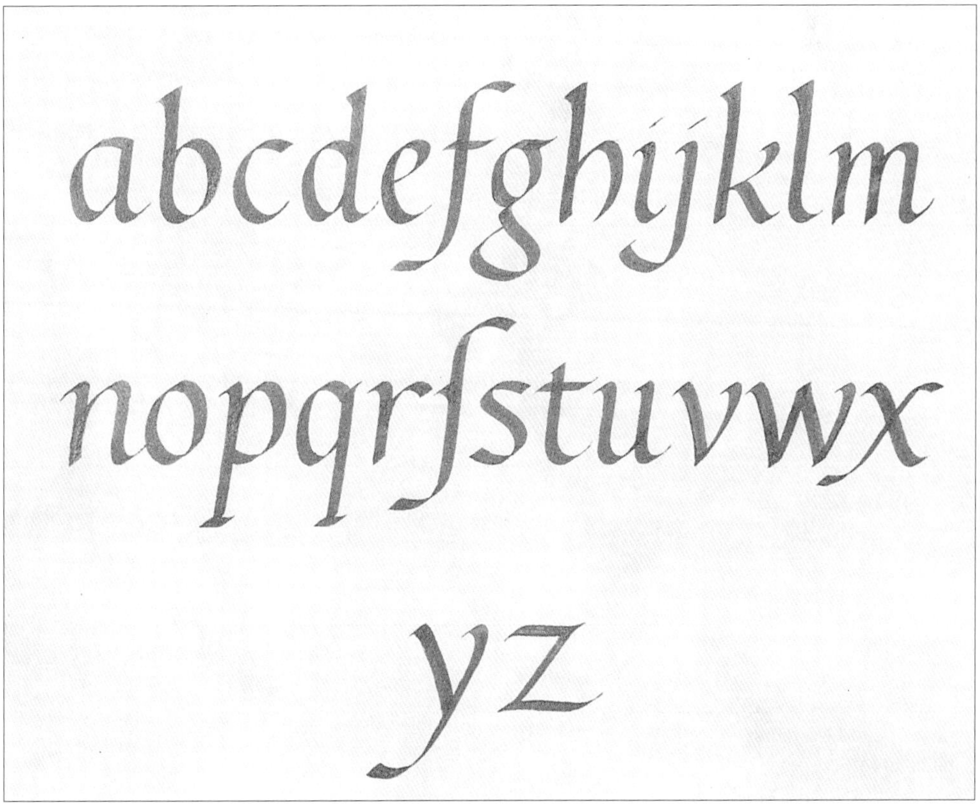

Figure 15: cancelleresca lettering.

abcdefghijklm
nopqrſstuvwx
yz

Figure 16: Line-fillers used with humanist antiqua.

Figure 17: Cancelleresca text with boxed Roman initial and decorative floral motifs.

Mirabile mysterium decla:
ratur hodie: irmouantur na:
turæ: Deus homo factus est:
id. quod fuit permasit:
et quod non erat. as:
sumpsit: non co:
mistionem
passus.
neq: dimsionem.

THE TROMPE-L'OEIL STYLE

Another very striking style of the Renaissance period was the development of letters and borders with a heavy, solid, background colour – particularly gold – with naturalistic objects strewn around the borders in a manner that has come to be known as trompe l'oeil (a French expression meaning 'deceives the eye'). The aim was to make the images that were painted on the background appear to be resting on, or projecting from, the page, and this was done by using shadow effects and modelling to create a three-dimensional effect. This style of illumination emerged from the fifteenth-century Flemish Ghent-Bruges school, from which it spread through France and Italy.

An early example of this style can be seen in the illuminated 'B' (Figure 18) which is taken from a breviary that was made in northern France in about 1525. (The manuscript, whose reference number is MS.Laud.misc.419, f.433r, is today owned by the Bodleian Library, Oxford University.) The scroll effect on the first stroke of the 'B' is a common feature of the trompe-l'oeil style. The pale outline of the letter combines with the sprouting branches in the curved parts of the letter's right-hand side, while the horizontal stems work their way back into the upright stroke to form the scrolls around the upright. The strawberry plant that forms the central decoration is painted in a semi-naturalistic manner. Smaller, slightly simpler initials in the same style, each contained within a square box, begin each verse of the text. The accompanying lettering is written in a Gothic style, which gives a slightly heavier effect than the humanist lettering that would later be associated with trompe l'oeil.

Figure 18: A trompe-l'oeil letter 'B' based on a French breviary dated 1525.

PROJECT: *Creating a trompe-l'oeil letter and border*

Figure 19 shows a piece commencing with an illuminated letter 'G'. The letter and text are surrounded by a full trompe-l'oeil border, in which an array of plants and creatures has been painted in a fine, naturalistic style.

Colours other than gold were sometimes used for the background, too. When designing a trompe-l'oeil piece, a green or a purple background can give an interesting effect, but red tends to be rather overpowering, while dark colours, such as brown and black, can look very sombre. You will find examples of all of these background colours in manuscripts of the period, however.

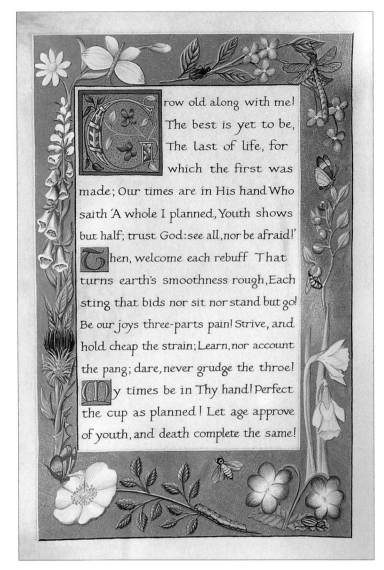

Figure 19: A trompe-l'oeil letter 'G' and border.

row old along with me!
The best is yet to be,
The last of life, for
which the first was
made; Our times are in His hand Who
saith 'A whole I planned, Youth shows
but half; trust God: see all, nor be afraid!'
    hen, welcome each rebuff That
turns earth's smoothness rough, Each
sting that bids nor sit nor stand but go!
Be our joys three-parts pain! Strive, and
hold cheap the strain; Learn, nor account
the pang; dare, never grudge the throe!
    y times be in Thy hand! Perfect
the cup as planned! Let age approve
of youth, and death complete the same!

| Make a complete draft of the text and border. The humanist-antiqua lettering needs to form a neat block to fill the central area. Rule the page margins and lines, then write the lettering.

2 Now trace the border design into place.

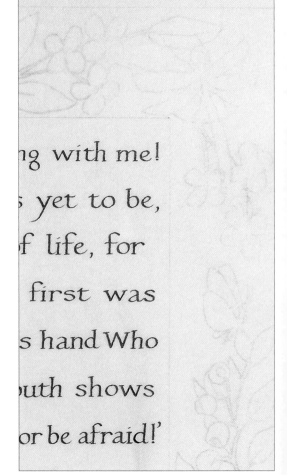

3 Paint the background with gold powder and then burnish it, leaving spaces for the plants and insects to be added afterwards.

4 The naturalistic modelling is painted with dry brushwork.

5 Build up each part of the letter and border with shading and highlighting to give as natural an appearance as possible.

6 Add dark and light outlines to the edges, as shown. The overall effect is of a very lavish mixture of gold and colours that contrasts strongly with the lightness and simplicity of the accompanying text.

Chapter 9

This book has provided an introduction to some of the
main types of illuminated letter, along with their
corresponding lettering styles, border work and
accompanying decorative details. However, there are countless
other examples and styles that you can use as starting points for
designing new pieces of work. For example, there was not the
scope in this book to cover rustica lettering, the Beneventan
script, the Visigothic or Lombardic styles or to explore the
Byzantine and Ottonian art forms and their influences or Islamic
manuscripts, which provide a wealth of wonderful designs and
attractive colour schemes.

In Britain, the British Library and the Victoria & Albert
Museum in London display many fine examples of illuminated
manuscripts, while numerous further manuscripts can be found
in museums throughout the world that you could draw on for
ideas and inspiration.

MODERN USES OF ILLUMINATION

There is great satisfaction to be drawn from developing new pieces from the study of historical examples. Contemporary designs based on such early originals have their own character and points of interest, and you can let your imagination wander in whichever direction you prefer.

Figures 1 and 2 show some designs for cards that are based on historical examples. Figure 3 shows a small piece that describes the meaning of a child's name, with an illuminated initial letter and border that were inspired by historical manuscripts.

Figure 1: A 'Noel' Christmas card.

Figure 2: A 'Greetings' card.

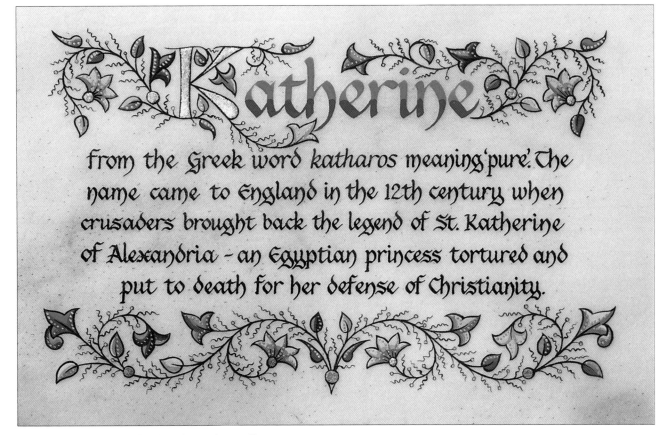

from the Greek word katharos meaning 'pure'. The name came to England in the 12th century when crusaders brought back the legend of St. Katherine of Alexandria - an Egyptian princess tortured and put to death for her defense of Christianity.

Figure 3: Top and bottom borders frame this small text.

PROJECT: *A 'Noel' Christmas card*

1 Begin by making a complete draft of the text and illuminated letter.

2 Cut a piece of card to the required size and write the pen-made letters into place. (A size 3 Automatic nib was used for this card.)

3 Trace the initial letter and decoration into place.

4 Work through the letter in the usual manner, with the gold areas being painted first, then the base colours and outlines, finally adding the modelling work and fine detail.

5 The written letters are given a darker overpainting to the bottom half. The design is then complete.

PROJECT: *A 'Greetings' card*

1 The draft of a Celtic 'greetings' card.

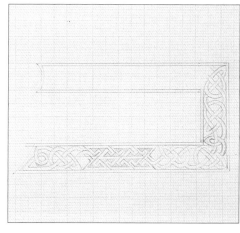

2 Work out the border design on graph paper if necessary.

3 Write the text into place on the card.

4 Paint the border in strong, vibrant colours.

5 The completed card.

PROJECT *An illuminated menu*

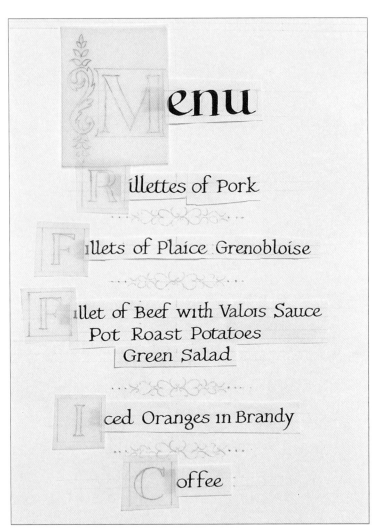

1 | Make a draft of the text and initial letters.

2 Write the text, then paint in the background colours of the initials.

3 Add line-fillers with a fine pen.

4 Final detail is added to the initials.

MOUNTING, FRAMING AND CARING FOR YOUR WORK

Take care of the pieces that you create by framing or storing them well. If a piece of work contains any sort of real gold powder or leaf, it should be framed with either a mount or a thin slip of wood between the glass and the work to prevent the glass from coming into contact with the gold, which it would damage.

Figure 4 shows a framed manuscript that is based on a page from the Bedford Psalter and Hours (dated about 1420 and now in the British Library). Because the work contains a large amount of raised gilding, a thin slip of wood has been incorporated into the frame, between the work and the glass, in such a way that it cannot be seen. The main frame was hand-painted in a cream colour to match the vellum on which the work was painted and to bring out the colours of the design. This particular frame had a rebate, or rabbet, large enough to take the glass and work, as well as the additional thickness of the wooden slip, but most good picture-framers can usually find a way in which to frame any depth of painting, mount board or slip, glass and backing board, even when the frame's rebate (Figure 5) is insufficiently large. The piece illustrated in Figure 6 has a dark frame with a gold-coloured, wooden slip between the glass and vellum. This time, the gold slip has been allowed to remain visible within the main frame, thereby making the whole frame appear wider.

Figure 4: This illuminated text, based on a page from the Bedford Psalter and Hours, is framed with a wooden slip between glass and frame to keep the glass from touching the raised gold.

Figure 5: A frame moulding showing the rebate.

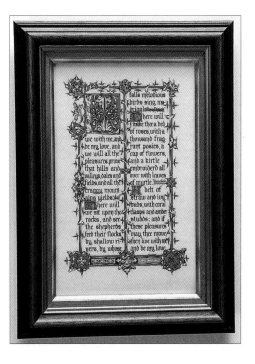

Figure 6: This piece is framed with a visible gold slip between the glass and artwork.

Mount board comes in a large range of colours, so it should be easy to find one that will suit your particular piece of work. You will sometimes have a choice of several thicknesses, in which case choose the thickest, because this will protect the work better. Some mount boards also have a grained, or laid, texture, which can look attractive (Figure 7). Picture-framers will cut mounts with bevelled edges to size for you, which look better than the straight-cut mounts that you can make yourself (Figure 8).

Provided that they are not too large, manuscripts or individual, richly illuminated letters can often benefit from quite large margins around the work (Figure 9). Alternatively, the mount can serve as the margin if it is taken quite close to the edge of the painting (Figure 10). If the piece contains detail that extends into the border and makes the work look unbalanced when it is centred, wider margins will help to make the artwork appear more centrally positioned within the frame (figures 11–12).

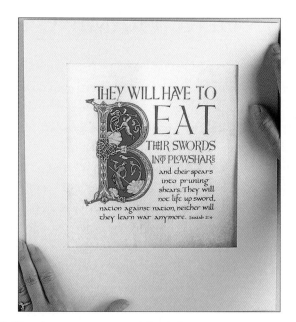

Figure 9: Allow large margins around detailed pieces.

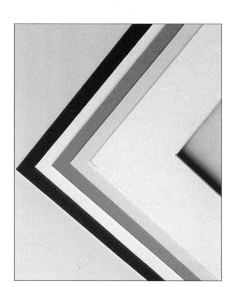

Figure 7: Mount board samples.

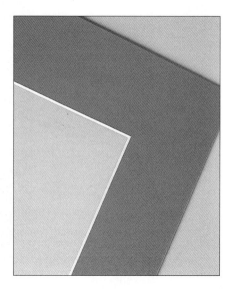

Figure 8: Bevelled edge to mount aperture.

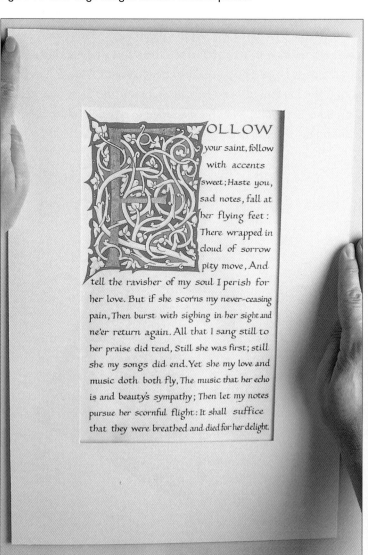

Figure 10: Mount board used as a margin.

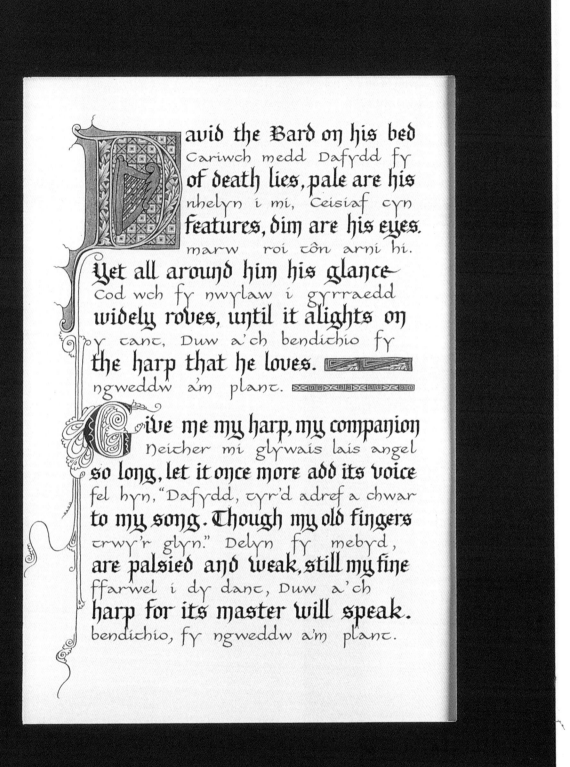

You should also remember that vellum will not remain flat if it becomes too warm (Figure 13), but will instead try to return to its original shape (when it was still part of a calf). It is likely that framed vellum will buckle. As long as it does not buckle too much, this is not really a problem – indeed, it can even add character to your manuscript – but try to avoid displaying framed vellum in an excessively warm site, for example, on a wall above a radiator or fire.

Never hang a piece of work in direct sunlight, which will fade non-light-fast colours very quickly and will also prematurely age the writing surface, whether it is vellum or paper (Figure 14). Instead, try to hang your work on a wall that receives no direct sunlight. Artificial light can be ideal for work that contains gilding, because light coming from different directions will highlight the gold beautifully as you move about examining the piece, and will really show it off to best advantage.

Another factor to consider is damp: mould can grow on vellum and paper if they are kept in very damp conditions. If this has happened to one of your pieces, it should be removed from its frame and treated before being reframed and hung in a dryer position. If the piece is greatly valued, employ or consult a professional picture-framer about the best cleaning process.

If the work has not been framed, look after it by keeping it laid flat – preferably not rolled up or folded – in acid-free tissue paper in a storage area that is free from damp. If you take it out to show people, explain that it is best not to touch it. People are fascinated by original artwork and will often want to touch the paint or gold – some may even try to rub it to see if it is real! Apart from any damage that they may do, however, people's fingers will always transmit a certain amount of grease and dirt to anything that they touch, even though their hands may appear to be perfectly clean. So before showing a piece to viewers, make sure that they understand that they can look, but not touch.

I hope that this book will provide an inspiration to many readers, and that it will encourage you to produce more illuminated pieces and thus keep a very beautiful art form alive.

Figure 12: Larger margins will help to centralise the text and decoration.

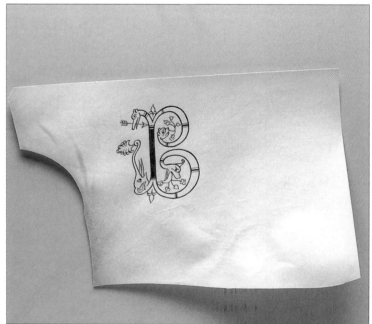

Figure 13: A piece of vellum will warp dramatically in the heat.

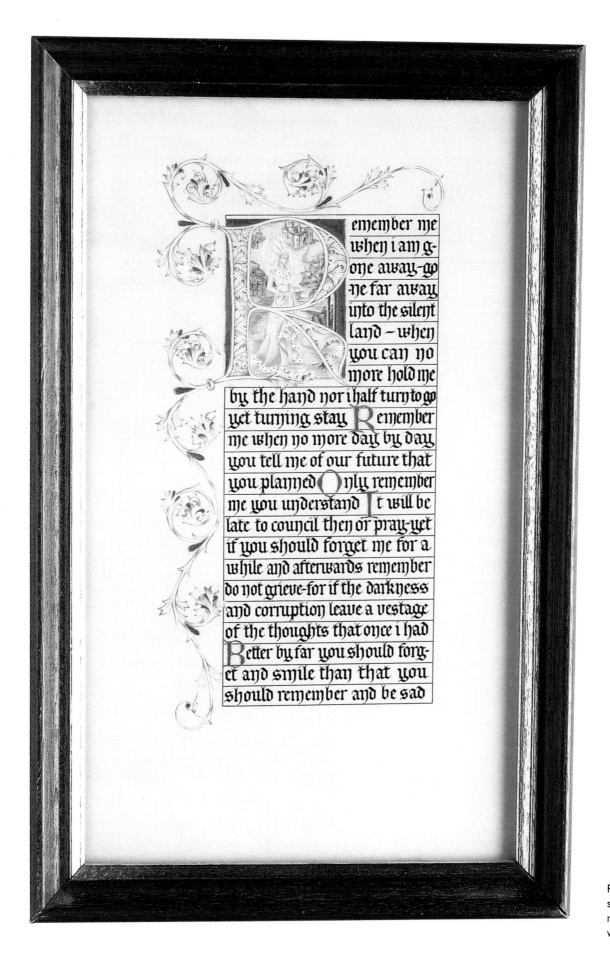

Figure 14: Direct sunlight will fade non-light-fast colours very quickly.

GLOSSARY

Acanthus:

a decorative foliage design based on the acanthus plant, much used during antiquity.

Anglo-Saxon:

the period from 500 to 1066 in England.

Anthropomorphics:

human forms used for decoration.

Antiphonal:

a manuscript containing the sung parts of the divine office.

Antiquity:

the classical period of Greek and Roman art, before the decline of the Roman Empire during the fifth century.

Ascender:

the part of a letter that extends above the top writing line.

Bas-de-page:

a scene at the bottom of the page.

Bestiary:

a book of beasts, real or imaginary.

Book of hours:

a book used for private devotions based on the divine office.

Breviary:

a manuscript containing texts used for the celebration of the divine office.

Burnish:

to polish or rub a surface to achieve a bright shine.

Burnisher:

a tool used to polish a surface.

Byzantine:

a style of painting that emanated from the Eastern city of Byzantium (later renamed Constantinople and then Istanbul), particularly from the ninth to the eleventh centuries.

Camaieu:

a painting in shades of a single colour.

Canticles:

short hymns.

Carpet page:

a large, decorated page of illumination covering most of the sheet.

Clarea:

a mixing medium for powdered pigment made from whisked egg white.

Counterchanged:

a design in two or more sections in which the colours and patterns are reversed in each portion.

Crazing:

a thin tracery of lines on a piece of raised gold due to the cracking of the gesso beneath.

Damp-fold drapery:

a style of painting that gives drapery the appearance of wet fabric clinging to the body.

Decorated initial:

an initial letter whose decoration does not represent any particular feature.

Descender:

the part of a letter that falls below the bottom writing line.

Diaper:

a pattern, usually repeating, spread over a surface as decoration.

Divine office:

the cycle of devotions made at eight prescribed periods during the day.

Drolleries:

amusing figures used in medieval art.

Dry brushwork:

a painting technique that uses minimal paint to give a blending effect.

Epistolary:

a service book containing the epistle readings for the mass.

Evangelary:

a manuscript containing the gospel readings for the mass.

Foliate-bar border:

a border based on a straight-edged framework decorated with flowers and foliage.

Folio:

a sheet of writing material.

Glair:

a mixing medium for powdered pigments made from whisked egg white.

Gothic:

a period, and style of illumination, between antiquity and the Renaissance, roughly dating from the late twelfth to the early sixteenth century.

Gradual:

the principal choir book used in the mass.

Grisaille:

a painting consisting solely of shades of grey.

Grotesques:

hybrid figures, usually composed of human and animal forms, and often having a comic character.

Herbal:

a book containing information about, and illustrations of, plants.

Historiated initial:

an initial letter containing a recognisable scene relating to a particular event.

Humanistic:

a style of painting that revived classical learning and originated in Florence, Italy.

Hymnal:

a manuscript containing the hymns sung in the divine office.

Inhabited initial:

an initial letter containing figures or creatures, but not in an identifiable scene.

Insular:

a period, and style of illumination, in Britain and Ireland between 550 and 900.

Key pattern:

a geometric pattern of interlocking shapes.

Knotwork:

a pattern made with a continuous weaving line, found particularly in Celtic art.

Kyriale:

a book containing the ordinary chants of the mass.

Line-filler:

a small piece of decoration used to fill space at the end of a line of text.

Littera florissa:

light, pen-worked decoration added to letters.

Liturgy:

the rites, observances and procedures of public worship.

Majuscule:

a capital or upper-case letter.

Mass:

part of the liturgy, the celebration of the Eucharist.

Minuscule:

a small or lower-case letter.

Missal:

a service book containing the texts used for the mass.

Modelling:

detail applied to a painting to achieve a sense of form.

Mortar:

a vessel in which substances are pounded or ground with a pestle.

Overpainting:

subsequent areas of paint on a background colour.

Parchment:

the skin of a sheep that has been prepared for writing or painting.

Pounce:

a powder used to clean and abrade the surface of vellum in preparation for writing or painting.

Psalter:

a book of psalms.

Romanesque:

a period, and style of illumination, in the Western world of the late eleventh and twelfth centuries, so called because it was based on Roman principles of construction.

Sacramentary:

a service book of prayers used during the mass.

Terminal:

the end point of a stroke of a letter or piece of decoration.

Trompe l'oeil:

'deceives the eye', a style of painting that attempts to give objects as naturalistic an appearance as possible.

Trope:

an early musical note.

Troper:

a book containing tropes.

Upright:

the vertical stroke of a letter.

Vellum:

the skin of a calf that has been prepared for writing and painting.

Zoomorphics:

animal forms used for decoration.

INDEX

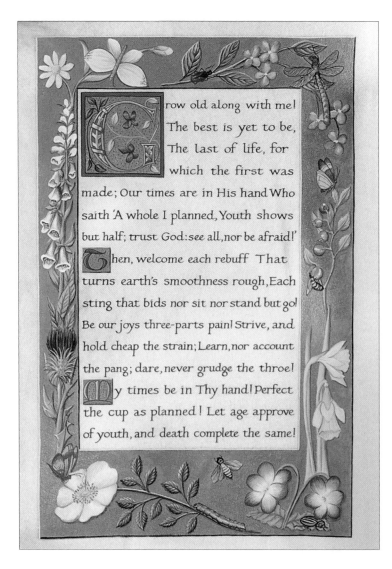